STORY MYTHOS

A Movie Guide to Better Business Stories

Shane Meeker
StoryMythos LLC

Illustrations by Rick Hagee

Speak It To Book
www.speakittobook.com

StoryMythos: A Movie Guide to Better Business Stories / Shane Meeker, StoryMythos LLC
ISBN-13: 978-1-945793-38-7
ISBN-10: 1-945793-38-4

Praise for *StoryMythos:*

A Movie Guide to Better Business Stories

I've long believed—and counseled—that the best and most memorable way for us to communicate our values and learnings is through stories—stories that link a principle of lasting importance to a specific event brought to life like it is a movie. You see it, you feel it, and you don't forget it. We don't tell enough stories, and we don't tell them as well as we should.

Shane Meeker's book *StoryMythos* addresses that reality by providing an illuminating, highly engaging tutorial on how to develop strong stories. Infused with sharp and relevant examples from movies, Walt Disney, and P&G, this book leaves one not only better appreciating the power of storytelling but knowing how to make it happen.

John Pepper, Former CEO of Procter & Gamble and Former Chairman of the Board of the Walt Disney Company

I have known and interacted with Shane for over a decade. This book represents the result of several years of experimentation with the power of myth and storytelling in a corporate context. It complements his educational and professional seminars and provides the road map for how we can make storytelling a valuable asset to building a brand and inspiring companies and consumers.

Craig M. Vogel FIDSA, Associate Dean for Graduate Studies and Research, College of DAAP, University of Cincinnati

A studious reader will be hard-pressed to find someone who can profess more eloquently the linkage between ancient story structures and pop culture narratives than Shane Meeker.

Utilizing his unique combination of detailed, highly polished articulations wrought from years of in-field practice and his authentic, playful "geek love" of contemporary film, Meeker masterfully weaves lesson after lesson around the dynamic power of storycraft. He does not cease to marvel us with how he can peel away new layers in the tales we thought we knew so well. Shane simply has no equivalent in industry or academia.

Joel Kashuba, Head of Design & Innovation, Fifth Third Bank

We're all made up of stories—but you know that. What you don't know is just how powerful stories can be for building your business/brand. Meeker provides a wildly insightful, entertaining, one-of-a-kind guide for helping you build your own brand story. You'll get a proven recipe for doing so, learn to control how your brand's story changes, how to leverage storytelling to decommoditize your brand, and how to make people care about/engage with your brand (and take action as a result). Meeker's skill in storytelling is put on full display with his vastly readable writing style. This is one story you'll quickly read straight through to The End.

***Scott Mautz, Author:* Find the Fire: Ignite your Inspiration & Make Work Exciting Again**

Over twenty-five years of driving significant organization and business transformation, nothing has been more important than being able to touch the heads and hearts to build action and momentum. Nothing does that better than being able to tell the story—your story, the transformation story, and the journey you want your team to take with you! I've participated in Shane's training now a half-dozen times; this book codifies the essence and will be a critical investment in your personal journey as a leader. Be the type of leader that changes the world and leaves your audience wanting more!

Andy Walter, VP Procter & Gamble (retired), Board Director & Strategic Advisor

The art of storytelling is the very fabric of human life and as old as mankind itself. It has framed our knowledge, our values, our principles and transferred our collective wisdom from generation to generation. Shane Meeker is the consummate master of the story, and his book the definitive guide to the creation of compelling narratives. A must read and reference text for anyone looking to build world-class communications skills.

Paul Fox, VP Procter & Gamble (retired), Visiting Fellow at The University of Oxford, and Principal, Derdale Consulting

If you ever wondered about the power of story to transform an

idea, a brand, or an organization, Shane shows how a great, human-centered story can move people, and, as a result, grow a business.
Holly O'Driscoll, Founder & CEO, Ampersand Innovation, LLC

Shane Meeker uses the Hollywood stories we know best to give us the leadership insights we need most. If I were to write the pitch for this book, I'd describe it as "Walt Disney meets Peter Drucker"—timeless stories and practical wisdom that can help you solve *any* business problem you're facing. You'll put this gem-of-a-book to use even before you finish reading it.
Greg Icenhower, President & Owner, Leader's Voice Communications

People forget PowerPoint slides. They remember carefully crafted stories. What Shane does with an innovative style, provides the reader with the ingredients to the secret sauce of storytelling. It's a must read if you want people to want more of your message.
Robert Sherwood, Regional Head, Human Resources, Givaudan Flavor Division

Dedicated to the most important part of my life's story, my lovely wife Regina and my three incredible boys—Calvin, Spencer, and Ian. You are the meaning and inspiration behind my Hero's Journey and the most important part of my story.

I also can't forget to say thanks to my childhood heroes who got me into the world of storytelling: Luke Skywalker, Captain Nemo, Batman, Walt Disney, and C. C. Deville.

I also have to thank my P&G mentors—Phil, Greg, Steve, Debbie, Emily, Tom, Alison, Martha, Michael, and Charlene. Without them I would have never become the P&G Corporate Storyteller. I am forever indebted to all of you for believing in me and taking a chance on my ideas.

A special thanks to Rick Hagee for the awesome illustrations and helping me create my brand and to Greg for early editing help and being an ear to bounce book ideas around.

Contents

INTRODUCTION

What This Book Is All About

In my twenty-one years working for the largest consumer products company in the world, I have yet to find a business problem that I could not solve with what I love about *Star Wars*—a great story.

Since I was a child, stories have always pushed my imagination, made me look at things differently, and helped me ask the important question "What if...?"

My job as the company historian and corporate storyteller at Procter & Gamble is to help our brands, project teams, and employees understand and leverage the power of *story* and use it as a tool to help solve a variety of challenges. Over the years, I have shared my story-based techniques across hundreds of initiatives and areas, such as disruptive innovation, brand development, organizational culture, team building, and creating communications.

Do you want to know the big secret behind my storytelling content? The secret behind all the tools and techniques that I share with teams?

Simple—it all comes from my love of movies. A way to use what works in stage, page, and screen as a strategic tool. This book is a movie guide to better business stories.

Everything I teach is inspired by what I learned as I was trying to write a screenplay many years ago. I have since taken what I love about my favorite books, TV shows, and movies and created a series of business presentations and workshops on story techniques.

A little different, I know. But I have yet to find a project that wouldn't benefit from a solid story.

Let me start our journey by asking a question.

Do you consider yourself an expert story builder or storyteller?

If "No," well, you are in good company. I often start my story presentations with that question, and almost 98 percent of the time, no one raises their hand. I share my story content and do story workshops over a dozen times a month across the globe with hundreds of companies, institutions, and conferences—places with incredibly talented people that boast impressive backgrounds and vast experience in marketing, communication, sales, engineering, and senior management.

Yet only a fraction of these people feel that they have true expertise in the craft of story.

That situation needs to be fixed, because story is *everything* in business.

But even if you answered "yes," you still need to practice and always work to improve your skills. You need to keep up with new story trends. The good news is that we all are familiar with the idea of stories—reading them, watching them, listening to them, or sharing them. In fact, I believe telling stories is what we were born to do. If there is one consistent thing that we all do in every corner of the world, it is telling stories.

A little much? Well, think about it this way.

You cherish your stories. You collect your stories. You protect your stories. And you even create and love to share your stories. Let's be honest, what will be left of you when you are gone someday? Simply the stories.

But just because we were born for stories does not make us great at creating them. Like anything else, it takes practice.

Teaching the art of story in the business world is often done too quickly, treated as a nonmandatory "one day" session—or worse, never done at all. "Story fundamentals" is not a core part of any MBA program I know of. What makes this lost art form even trickier to master is that there is no single class or book that can transform you, your employees, or your organization overnight. Great storytelling—whether around a campfire or in the business world—takes a passionate dedication to master, and mastery takes time.

I wrote this book to help get you started. I hope

if nothing else it inspires you to explore the world of "story" and why storytelling is one of the most powerful human skills.

The tools and ideas I will share in these pages are ones that I developed after watching thousands of movies and then working with thousands of people and teams around the world. By the end, I hope you will see how the stories you love, regardless of what they are, arm you with unique insights that can take your day-to-day business to a whole new level.

I want to unleash that brilliant, creative storyteller who's already inside of you. And don't look at the floor or blush as you read that. Accept it.

You. Are. A. Storyteller.

Everyone is! Maybe the creative storyteller within you has just fallen asleep and needs to be reawakened, much like Gordon Mackenzie talks about in his brilliant book *Orbiting the Giant Hairball* (if you haven't yet, read that book!).

Creativity can be an unfortunate casualty of a business world dead set on finding normalcy through numbers, formulas, and analytics. Although these things are vital to any business, they tend to choke out the creative genius in us all. And when that happens, an incredible power is lost. Think of it like this:

You could share with your team how many hours your company collectively helped volunteer at a local shelter or you could let them tell their personal stories about what it means to help others. Which would reach people at a deeper and more emotional level?

Now, to yield this awesome power, you first have to understand what a story is.

What is a "story," anyway?

Just Google "brand story" and you're going to get millions of hits. "Story" has become the latest buzzword in business vocabulary today. What makes matters worse—and, quite frankly, *annoying*—is that the business world often talks about storytelling as if it's some *new* tool or method just now being discovered and focused on. Instead of being honored and explored, in many cases it's being buzzworded to death just like "brand equity," "purpose," "agility," and "innovation."

Like a song played too often on radio, storytelling can become diluted in our minds. Even cartoons like *Dilbert* have poked fun at its overuse in business and potentially sapped meaning.

But story is not a choice. Your business cannot avoid the reality of story any more than it can avoid the reality of innovation: without it, a company suffers.

Storytelling is simply what humans do, which means storytelling is what your business does. Most companies understand this and acknowledge story's importance. Where they fail, however, is in trying to treat story like a checkbox, formula, or algorithm.

Trust me, I get it. Who doesn't like a clear checklist or a formula for how to do something?

But as we've learned from Aristotle to Shakespeare to Joseph Campbell to Steven Spielberg, story is different. A story is living and breathing—it's *emotive*, and it's happening within us all.

To understand this, recognize it, and *live it* takes a different kind of practice—the art of knowing people. There's no formula that will consistently bring back how you felt when you were a wide-eyed child and your favorite books and movies mesmerized and transported you to fantastic new worlds and ideas. That journey to the past takes practice of a different kind, and even the masters at story still fail sometimes. That is because emotion is not a formula. But, as with anything, research and practice always helps.

That's what I plan to teach in the coming chapters—ideas and concepts to help you ponder and practice.

What this book will and won't do for you

Reading this book will not make you an expert storyteller, but I hope it becomes a resource for you, a tool, and I hope it inspires you to take even more steps in learning the art of story.

As you read—and respond to the application

questions in the workbook segments that follow most chapters—keep an open mind. Remember that this book is just one person's thoughts, feelings, and ideas. It's based on my opinions and experiences. There are so many great story experts and resources out there, so check them all out! Make sure you see, hear, and learn other ideas from other authors in other books and articles.

A lot of my content was inspired and influenced by other story experts and writers. Everything is a remix of something else. You see and learn something, then add your ideas to it so that it is transformed into something new. The power of serendipity. Do that with this book, too.

> A good artist knows that nothing comes from nowhere. All creative work builds on something that came before. Nothing is completely original.[1]
>
> **—Austin Kleon, *Steal Like an Artist***

CHAPTER ONE

Start with Your Personal Story

> No two people will experience life the same, so no two people will tell a story the same way. Think of this as a superpower we all have, your unique perspective.[2]
>
> **— Valerie Lapointe, PIXAR**

When I lead story workshops with teams or brands, I don't want to write their stories—it's *their* story. I just want to help them find the story, to unlock the story, to help pull it from their hearts and minds, and to show them the deeper meaning behind it. I am simply there to help.

This is what a corporate storyteller should aim to do. Like the old saying,

> Give a man fish and he eats for a day, teach a man to fish and he eats for a lifetime.

I often start my story sessions by asking people

to share a quick story about themselves.

Who are you? What is your story? What story would you tell me so that I would better understand who you really are?

This is where our journey together begins. I want you to get to know me a little better. Let's start with why I love stories so much.

What's my story: Where am I coming from?

I have been around movies my entire life. Watching movies was just part of my family's normal weekend activity. When I was a kid, we had an old 8mm movie projector and a couple of silent film reels of *Spiderman* cartoons, a couple scenes from *Star Wars*, a short *Droopy* cartoon, and a few obscure family recordings. I particularly loved one in which my dad and his friends reenacted a classic movie scene of explorers bound to a bamboo pole by angry natives—ready to be burned—but then cleverly escaped.

When my parents pulled that projector out every couple of months, a grin always stretched across my entire face and I geared up for popcorn movie night—a night of escape, fantasy, and fun right in our own living room!

The interesting thing, though, is that there was no sound in these films—*and it didn't matter*. We all loved the experience of the stories. A picture is worth a thousand words, right?

Then, of course, came a great device called a VCR. Now that brought a whole new WOW factor! Full picture and sound with hundreds of films to choose from (paltry selection compared to what we have now, but incredible back then). We couldn't afford to own a VCR right away, so we would occasionally rent one from a local grocery for a weekend.

What an incredible treat that was, and I always asked for the same movies—*Star Wars, Raiders of the Lost Ark,* and *20,000 Leagues Under the Sea*. I must have seen those three films hundreds of times.

When we finally owned a VCR, the Friday trip to the video rental store became a regular treat. Bringing your favorite movies to the comfort of your home was just incredible!

I loved books too. Sci-fi, fantasy, and comic books were a nightly bedtime habit. As a kid, I always had a bookshelf in my room, and it was full with whatever my "classics" were at the time. The *Berenstain Bears and the Spooky Old Tree* was one of my all-time favorite adventure books when I was a little kid—a tree with a mysterious dungeon below it that needed to be explored. Who wouldn't want to be part of that?

Later, as a teen, I got into Jules Verne, H. G. Wells, J.R.R. Tolkien, Stephen King, and Dean Koontz. My dad also liked King and Koontz, and anytime he was reading one of their books, he would share it campfire-style with my brother and me while we drove somewhere. Car time was often story time. The moral and meaning behind this—this story of my childhood—is that I always knew that creating stories would need to be a part of my life. Sure enough, it became my full-time job.

Music is also a huge part of my story. I listen to music every day. I love the power that music can have. Songs tell a story and so do the notes. Music has always been an inspiration for me and a comfort when I need it.

When I feel bad, I turn on the music.

When I feel great, I crank up the music!

Funny, my musical taste hasn't changed much since the 80s. I still listen to a lot of hair metal—bands like Cinderella, Def Leppard, Skid Row, Warrant, and Mötley Crüe. One of my favorite 80s bands would change my life by inspiring me to learn the guitar. The band was called Poison. One Saturday morning when I saw the music video for the Poison song "Nothin' but a Good Time" on MTV, I said to myself, "That is what I want to do with my life…be a rock guitarist!"

C. C. Deville, the guitarist for Poison, was my idol. I wanted to play like him so badly. I spent countless hours learning every Poison song note by note. I never gave up. I quickly found myself in bands (the first one was called Jester) and have been with different bands ever since. Because I played, my younger brother wanted to learn too, and we eventually played in a couple of bands together (which were my favorites). All three of my kids are in music, and two of them asked me to teach them how to play guitar. Now one of them is in a band with me.

I have been a guitarist for over thirty years now, helped people close to me fall in love with the guitar, and been in over half a dozen bands—all because I saw a Poison video one morning. There is a story here, and with a story there should always be an insight. A moral or meaning. For this one it is the old saying that *"even the smallest things can have a big impact."* Who knew a single music video could have so much influence?

The stories that shaped who I am

Childhood stories like these made me who I am today. What about you?

The more you understand what influenced and guided you to becoming who you are, the more you'll understand the great power of a story. It will also help you understand the meanings behind the stories, what they are *really* about.

Stories, through the vehicle of emotion, create

change and transformation in us. Adventure, imagination, excitement, and discovery are all so important. But of all the stories I have encountered, a single movie proved the most life altering.

I saw it in 1977, and it was called *Star Wars*.

Star Wars *and me*

I remember the first time I saw *Star Wars* at the theater. I can still see that incredible first scene with the Star Destroyer zooming overhead attacking the fleeing rebel ship. It was the summer of 1977, and I, like many kids, was an adventure-seeking, starry-eyed child who wanted to change the world.

The main character in the film wanted to find adventure and change the world too; his name was Luke Skywalker. I could relate to Luke, I wanted to be him, and in many ways, I became Luke as I sat in the theater.

There were *so* many cool worlds, ships, and robots in that movie. After *Star Wars,* I was always inventing new laser guns, building models, or piecing together spaceship cockpits out of scrap cardboard. I mean, you can't be Luke if you don't have a cardboard ship in your room.

My parents always encouraged my "tinkering." My grandfather used to take me out to his barn, put a bucket of old machine parts, a couple 2×4 pieces, a hammer, a screwdriver, and some nails in front of me, and off I would go creating a futuristic weapon, a cardboard Batmobile, a tool for interstellar communications, or maybe part of a droid.

So, there I was in 1977, in the theater, watching what is probably the greatest sci-fi film of all time. I sat there mesmerized for two hours, on the edge of my seat for the entire movie. Behold, an entire new world was being opened for me, and one of my first reactions as I left the theater, smiling and full of ideas, was to get home and quickly continue the story.

I wanted to recreate it, but on my terms, with my own versions of the adventure, my own sequels and prequels. My imagination was set free because of this new world.

I got these cool things called "action figures," made homemade spaceships (using LEGOs, shoeboxes, and some of my engineer dad's old punch card computer equipment), and basked in the great rural Ohio landscape (vine draping willow trees, root cellars, and a good sandbox) where I had all I needed to create an immersive, dramatic story in my own galaxy, far, far away.

I hope, like me, that your childhood makes you smile too. I wouldn't change a thing. I am a product of my childhood, and I am very proud of that. That doesn't mean it didn't have its share of trouble and tragedy, but even those really help you understand the power of the story.

In a 2015 video on leadership created by *The Washington Post*, Paul Polman, CEO of Unilever, said that *"...in the Netherlands we simply say don't forget your house number, don't forget where you came from,"* meaning you should never forget where and how you grew up. It's a huge part of who you are today.[3]

How Star Wars *got me drawing*

One of the other things that *Star Wars* did for me was to inspire me to start drawing. Every day, over and over, blank sheet after blank sheet, I feverishly put pencil to paper. I wanted to recreate those fantastic spaceships and monsters I'd seen and then create *new* mysterious worlds and futuristic technologies. The more I practiced, the better I got, and soon I drew every day, creating new creatures, ships, and battle scenes.

I often would give my drawings to my mom and dad or send them to my grandparents. There is nothing like getting your drawings hung on the fridge when you're a kid—that is better than any NYC art show. As my skills grew, I soon realized that what I really wanted to do was work for Industrial Light & Magic someday (the company that did the special effects for *Star Wars*). I wanted to come up with those cool ships and droids for the movies.

But the more I drew, the more I also came to realize that I was still missing something.

Even though I could think up wild ideas, I couldn't always make them come to life the way I saw them in my head. I was missing a lot of fundamentals in taking drawing to the next level, concepts like perspective, shadow, and dimensionality. So, my parents got me bunches of instruction books and put me in a couple of classes—anything to help me learn. A day didn't go by that I wasn't sketching something. All year long I would draw.

How drawing got me into industrial design and P&G

Years later, while in college at The Ohio State University, I learned that my passion for creating new ideas and drawing could be used in a career called industrial design. Soon I had earned a degree in industrial design, and that was what I did for fifteen of my twenty-one years at P&G.

I led the design strategy and execution on billion-dollar brands such as Tide, Downy, Dawn, Cascade, Pampers, and Olay. I worked on upstream and downstream projects, brand extensions, and totally new product forms, applying my passion for aesthetics, functionality, and ergonomics into hundreds of different products and packages.

Then about ten years ago I started teaching the fundamentals and principles of story and storytelling inside and outside of P&G. Shortly after that, the company created a position for me called "corporate storyteller."

Star Wars led to drawing, drawing led to industrial design, industrial design led to P&G, and my lifelong love of movies led to becoming the P&G corporate storyteller and historian.

My job now is to protect, share, and bring to life the company history both internally and externally, while also teaching and leading the idea of story—all because a little kid watched and found himself enamored by a film called *Star Wars*. Stories connect things. What connections are in yours?

How P&G got me a chance to work on Star Wars

During my first internship at P&G, I met a designer who introduced me to a friend he had at ILM (Industrial Light & Magic). Yep, the company I wanted to work for when I was a little kid. You expect great connections when you work for a world-famous company, but this took "great connection" to a whole new level for me. Industrial Light & Magic!

After a couple meetings with some folks at ILM, I was able to do my college senior project with one of their lead concept artists, exploring different designs for a small droid that was being added to the 1997 *Star Wars: Episode IV* rerelease. While none of my ideas ended up making it to the film (darn), I still got to draw and create ideas for *Star Wars*— talk about full circle (and the artist I worked with gave me some

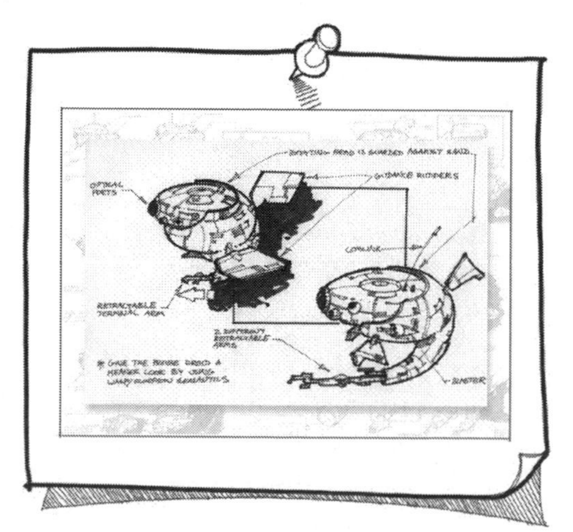

of his incredible movie concept sketches)!

It's funny how life works. Like my guitar story, there is a deeper meaning behind this one, too.

It is that the most important things in life are the connections you make with others. When you tell a story, always ask yourself what the moral to the story is. That will help you decide how to tell it and which parts are the most important to share. Knowing the moral helps you decide what to keep and what you could cut. That works in presentations, notes, and even PowerPoint slides.

Stories are windows into who we are

To know people, you have to learn about and understand the stories that are important to them. Our protected and cherished stories are windows into who we are and what's important to us. If you want to get to know someone, ask them which childhood stories were instrumental in making them who they are today.

I think our most formative years are from kindergarten to college graduation.

The places you lived, books you read, TV shows you watched, movies you loved, music you listened to, schools you attended, subjects you enjoyed, friends you had, accomplishments you earned, failures you grew from, mentors who inspired you, tragedies you endured, causes you believed in, your family, hobbies, faith, and spirituality—all of these are a part of your story and who you are today.

What's most important from these questions, though, is discussing what those things did *to you* and what actions they caused and how they brought about change. That is the real story. It's not about *Star Wars* for me. It's what *Star Wars* sparked in me—that is my story's *truth.*

Joseph Campbell, the great comparative mythologist who wrote one of my favorite books, *The Hero with a Thousand Faces*, has a few great quotes on this:

> Sit in a room and read—and read and read. And read the right books by the right people. Your mind is brought onto that level, and you have a nice, mild, slow-burning rapture all the time.[4]
>
> **—Joseph Campbell**

Sparks and catalysts for ideas and change form through the stories you digest.

> People say that what we're all seeking is a meaning for life. I don't think that's what we're really seeking. I think that what we're seeking is an experience of being alive, so that our life experiences on the purely

> physical plane will have resonances with our own innermost being and reality, so that we actually feel the rapture of being alive.[5]
>
> **—Joseph Campbell**

And one more.

> ...if you do follow your bliss, you put yourself on a kind of track that has been there all the while, waiting for you, and the life you ought to be living is the one you are living.[6]
>
> **—Joseph Campbell**

All stories are about life. Story is not a formula, but instead a form—a form for sharing and expressing the world with all of its passions, problems, solutions, people, and purpose.

So how have I been able to solve all the business problems I've worked on with what I love about *Star Wars*? Because *Star Wars* is about life. It is all about recognizing and feeling a hero's struggles and desires: facing and overcoming challenges, realizing purpose, finding allies and mentors, discovering new skills, and uncovering powerful treasures that not only transform the hero but also entire groups of people.

It was all of that for Luke.

It is for any great brand or company today.

And it's my story, too.

WORKBOOK

Chapter One Questions

Question: What experiences and stories from your childhood were instrumental in shaping who you are today: ones that you protect and cherish because they are important to you?

Question: What is the moral or deeper meaning to each of those stories?

Chapter One Notes

CHAPTER TWO

The Power of Story

Even though I loved the world of design, I always wanted to try my hand in Hollywood. I wanted to write a movie. I think every movie lover thinks of writing a screenplay at some point. Almost nineteen years ago, I had a screenplay idea and I started to write. I worked on it feverishly, but it just wasn't there. Something wasn't clicking, and I quickly realized what it was—I had no idea what I was doing! I didn't have any experience writing a screenplay!

Just like when I was a kid learning to draw, I had the ideas and the passion but was missing the craft. Just because I had watched thousands of films didn't mean I could write one! I needed to do research and then once again practice what I learned.

Many years later, I read a book that explained the importance of practice. It was Malcolm Gladwell's book *Outliers*. I hope you've had the pleasure of reading it, because it should be mandatory reading in the business world. Its pages provoke a simple question: "What makes someone an expert?"[7]

Gladwell researched and examined experts across a wide variety of fields and found that most experts had a couple things in common.

The first? How much passion they had for what they did.

The second? Practice. *Lots* of practice.

Gladwell was even able to quantify how many hours of practice were needed to call yourself an expert: 10,000 hours.[8]

Now, to be clear, that is not 10,000 hours of meeting about it, strategizing it, pontificating on it, or discussing it. Emails don't count here (unless you want to be an expert email writer). That is 10,000 hours of actually rolling your sleeves up and doing it.

Even though I had an idea for a screenplay, I had not put in even close to 10,000 hours of practice writing one. So, for the next several years, I started doing extensive research into the world of story, of writing, and with that came *lots* of practice.

I explored subjects like mythology, cultural anthropology, story psychology, history, fairy tales, legends, and journalism. I studied experts like Shakespeare, Syd Field, Robert McKee, Aaron Sorkin, Vladmir Propp, Annette Simmons, Christopher Vogler, Ed Catmull, Walt Disney, and story philosophers like Aristotle and Joseph Campbell. I built a vast story research library in my house and I still add new books to it every month.

I sank my teeth into all things related to story, analyzing anything I could get my hands on. And after thousands and thousands of hours of reading, taking classes, writing, sharing, and discussing, I realized something profound: all of it could be applied to the business world in simple and powerful ways.

Stories are not just for entertainment

Story was *not* only for the world of entertainment. It was also for the areas of business strategy, innovation, brand purpose, and holistic product experiences.

Brands, companies, and products quickly took on a very different light for me. Consumers became valiant heroes and brands became wise mentors, bestowing magical items called products that would help those heroes on their journeys.

I realized that if a brand, company, or product didn't have a good story—know it, understand it, and live by it—then it didn't really have anything.

Products don't really last—but the stories and people behind them do. Any company can copy a product or technology, but you just can't simply copy a great brand story.

Knowing this, I created a set of presentations, tools, and workshops that I call StoryMythos (meaning "a set of beliefs about story"). For over a decade now, I've been speaking and teaching both inside *and* outside of Procter & Gamble across over 100 different companies, conferences, and universities.

What began as 10 percent of my job is now my full-time job and my own company.

I have been a keynote speaker and shared my story content at companies like Walt Disney, American Express, Columbia Sportswear, Anheuser Busch, Lockheed Martin, and Exxon Mobil. I've taught story classes at colleges like The Ohio State University, the University of Michigan, and the University of Cincinnati. I am an adjunct professor at IIT in Chicago and teach story methodology to graduate students. My approach to using story in branding and innovation has been featured in many articles and in Cagan & Vogel's book *Creating Breakthrough Products: Revealing the Secrets that Drive Global Innovation* (second edition).

Finally, as the P&G company historian and corporate storyteller, I am also tasked with sharing and protecting the stories of the rich 180-year history of P&G and to making our heritage stories a strategic asset to inspire future generations by letting them look through the past.

All the research, presenting, speaking, writing, and workshops were just helping me get my 10,000 hours.

Now, that doesn't mean the learning stops. It just

means you've reached a new level of opportunity where you start to see your area of expertise differently and how you can take it to the next level.

I learn more about story every day, and I keep a running journal of all that I learn. I consistently change and add to my story presentation every couple of months. It's in a constant state of evolution because great stories should be. I try out new story tools and modules. Some work and some don't. Anytime I find a book on story, I read it; a video, I watch it; a speech, I listen to it; a podcast, I download it. I am constantly looking for opportunities to learn more.

You have to dig so deep into your passions that they become an extension of you. The key to doing so? Dedication—never letting up and never assuming that you've arrived. There is *no* end. It has to be ongoing. The world of story is always changing. It is honestly a lot like playing an instrument. Start building a story library in your office or home right now. Collect helpful books, save ideas, take notes, and sign up for some classes. Ask your manager for some time each week to sit and study. An hour here or a couple hours there. Report your findings back to your team at weekly meetings. Present your thoughts and ideas in front of people every chance you get. To help you get your library started, I will include a list of my favorite books in the Appendix.

So, after all that study, after reading all those

books and taking all those classes, I found the secret to a great story...the formula for a guaranteed hit.

Story is not a formula

Unfortunately, the short answer is that there isn't one. You can't codify emotion. This is a mistake many businesses can make. That is like trying to make all snowflakes the same.

As I said earlier, story isn't a formula. It is a form, a way of looking at and thinking about problems, and a way of seeing life. But most importantly, it is always subjective and personal. Trying to codify story would be like trying to codify humor. Just do this, this, and that, then everyone will laugh at all the same parts, right? Wrong. It doesn't work that way. Remember that movie your friend told you they couldn't stop laughing at so you went and saw it but barely cracked a smile?

Story is about personal connection and emotion, and those things are incredibly difficult to predict and measure. This is why the way we tell stories must be ever-evolving. It is also why even story masters can create bad ones too.

This is also why many businesses struggle with the idea of story.

Businesses tend to be pulled into what Gordon MacKenzie called "the hairball":

> A hairball is an entangled pattern of behavior. It's bureaucracy, which doesn't allow much space for original thinking and creativity. It's the corporate tendency to rely on past policies, decisions, and processes, as a formula for future success.[9]
>
> **—Gordon MacKenzie**

The word that causes trouble here is "formula." Stories don't have a formula because stories are emotion, and there is *no* formula for emotion. The good news is that the best brands and businesses know that story is incredibly important—they want it, strive for it, need it, can create it, and some are very good at it, but many still struggle with it. Why? One big reason is that the business world is often built around quantitative data, analytics, and predictive algorithms. Businesses crave data.

The golden goose in business is the ability to plug in X, add Y, and know that it will create Z—consistently, predictably, and measurably.

Alas, story does not work that way—and, as you'll see, that's a very good thing.

Story is about human emotions

Is every movie a well done, deep, powerful, and emotional story? Definitely not! That is because creating an emotional, shared experience is hard to do. Great stories are personal and they are human.

Don't make the mistake of turning people into numbers. Don't even talk that way inside your company. It's dangerous. Nobody wants to be seen as just a number.

Story touches your head and heart

Why do you re-watch some films, read some books over and over, and keep watching *Seinfeld* even though there hasn't been a new episode since 1998? Why do you watch *The Shawshank Redemption* over and over, even though you know the big reveal?

It's because they touch your head and heart in a way that is so special that you can't ignore it. You want to relive it, to feel it again. It's the same reason why I get excited every time I hear about a new Apple product!

Do people feel the same about your brand media, your commercials, and your content? What about inside your company? Are people "re-watching" your PowerPoints? Are they asking to get copies of your reports so they can read them again and share with their friends and family? When they ask for a copy of your work, can you see a light in their eyes—a spark, a signal that you have "touched" them in some way? Are people quoting your "lines" in the hallways like they quote their favorite movies?

We have all had presentations that people ask for copies of and we all have had presentations that no one wanted afterward. What was different? I will bet the first one had a great story. By the way, when anyone asks for a copy of your presentation, try and understand why. That is a great opportunity to go deeper and understand what you did that really made a difference.

Follow the trends set by story industries

Let's do a quick exercise. Go ahead and write down five of your favorite stories:

1.

2.

3.

4.

5.

So, what did you write? Chances are that you

wrote down some of your favorite TV shows, books, or movies. I really didn't ask for that, though. I said "favorite stories" (a bit of a loaded question, I know). The word "story" often takes you down that road, though. After all, when you were a kid and your teacher or parent said it was "story time," what did they read? An annual report? Of course not. Usually it was something from the field of stage, page, or screen.

For that reason, those industries are the first places I would recommend you study the craft of story. Those tales often represent society's mirrors. They show us what is being talked about and unique ways those messages can be expressed.

If you're the head of a business or organization, you need to understand the current hit stories. As a manager, you need to make a point of keeping up with the hit films, books, and TV shows. Remember, your employees, your teams, and your colleagues are watching and reading them. Many of them may be following the same stories you are. The popular ones become part of the cultural lexicon and of general conversations.

Look at this picture from Tire Discounters. They

felt that enough people followed and understood the story *Game of Thrones* to work a plot point into their advertisement!

Keeping up with the trends in brand media doesn't just mean watching commercials. Where do you think the agencies that created those ads get their inspiration? Even if you are creating an internal company communication, you need to understand the current trends in story to know how best to bring it to life. Every great company has powerful stories to tell. How you tell those stories matters a great deal.

One of my favorite stories to tell to new P&G employees is the origin story of the Tide detergent brand. It's a story that reinforces the old morals that nothing worthwhile is easy, that you need to be tenacious, learn from failure, and that it's important to have a manager who gives you space to try new things.

The story of the Tide brand

Back in the 1930s, a scientist named David Byerly[10] was tasked to develop what would later be called a "heavy duty detergent." He was a brilliant young scientist, known for his tenacity and his "take the bull by the horns" style. He was also known as a bit of a handful by his managers.

So, let's call him *very* determined!

Given his track record of great innovation, tenacity, and problem-solving, his management thought he would be the perfect one to develop this new product.

Up until that point, most laundry products were soap-based. And soap, although pretty good at cleaning, had drawbacks. For one thing, soaps don't form suds well in hard water, and suds are the key signal of efficacy. Second, real soap leaves behind a deposit in fabrics called *soap curd*, or *soap scum*, which over time can make clothes stiff and even turn them a little grey.

It was a very blue-collar time period in the United States; most people worked outdoors or got dirty at work, so there were a lot of very hard stains to deal with. Laundry was a tedious, labor-intensive task, and "washday" was not a short or easy chore.

P&G knew that a heavy-duty detergent could potentially fix these problems. Dreft, in 1933, was a step in the right direction, but it was a "light duty detergent," meaning it fixed some of those soap problems minus one—taking out the most difficult stains.

David and his team called the initiative Project X. But after seven years of failed experiments, the project was canceled by senior management and David was moved to another project, a very important one that was the result of a large-scale global conflict.

WWII had started, and the US Government

needed some of the chemicals that P&G used for its products. David was tasked with developing alternative chemistries that P&G could use during the war.

But he was also determined to keep Project X alive and to find the perfect solution to the stain problem.

He approached his manager and told him that he could do it, he knew he could, but that he just needed more time. His manager believed in him, and even though senior management had specifically canceled the project, he told David he could continue working on it as long as he was getting the WWII project done as well.

This was his "Google passion project" fifty-plus years before anyone knew what that was. (At Google, employees can dedicate 20 percent of their work plan to personal passion projects, of which many have grown into full-on company initiatives.)[11]

The one thing David's manager asked of him was to not include anything about Project X in his biweekly reports. David agreed, and he went back to the drawing board.

Years went by, and David continued to work through struggle after struggle. In fact, by year nine, he still had nothing but failure. But at year eleven, he had his first breakthrough, and he was so excited that he wanted to share it. He decided to write about it in his biweekly report.

Of course, senior management saw it and immediately went to David's manager asking why he was still working on a project that had been canceled over four years ago. They told his manager, "You have to stop this right now," because there were pressing issues at the plant and no time for this project. But his manager, having faith in David's tenacity and passion, told him to continue pressing on, but to please not put anything in future reports.

Eventually, David had a huge breakthrough and finally developed a heavy-duty detergent prototype to share—a full fourteen years after he'd started!Its cleaning power was unparalleled. No one had ever seen anything like it. It absolutely amazed Research and Development's senior management, and they immediately wanted to show it to the company president, Richard Deupree. The team piled into a car and went to the downtown P&G headquarters with the product demo in hand. Richard was amazed with the product and said he wanted it ready for the public in less than two years.

Tide launched in 1946, was the market leader by 1949, and has never left that position. It tripled the company's bottom line in under ten years. It was called the "Washday Miracle" because it helped eliminate the traditional washday.

Tide helped change the world, and it's all because of a scientist's passion to help the consumer, the tenacity to keep experimenting even after encountering failure, and a manager who understood how important it was to trust his employees.[12]

If you are not failing, then you are not innovating. David Byerly understood that. If you are a manager, you have to know what your people are capable of and give them the space to unleash their potential. David's manager really got that, and so did a more modern-day legend named Steve Jobs, who said, *"It doesn't make sense to hire smart people and then tell them what to do; we hire smart people so they can tell us what to do."*[13]

People are inspired and moved by stories

What are your most powerful company stories, and how are you using them to inspire your people? How do you explain your purpose through different stories? What stories best demonstrate your company beliefs? How are you documenting and protecting the stories that matter?

At the P&G Heritage Center, I often share a quote from a 1950s P&G Research and Development VP named J. G. Pleasants: *"No company can afford the luxury of rediscovering its own prior knowledge."*[14]

People are willing to dedicate themselves and their time to building and being part of great stories. Many people will even devote decades of their lives to a company if there's a story that they see their role in and want to be a part of. I know I have. People are always willing to follow great stories.

As I thought about one of my favorite book series, *Harry Potter*, I realized something: because I read each book as it was launched (which was about a year or two apart) that means I spent over a tenth of my probable lifespan following Harry and his adventures. That is incredible!

Similarly, I have followed *Star Wars* for most of my life—almost forty years! I kept up with its characters, read the news, looked forward to the future stories, felt anticipation and excitement as announcements were made, bought the merchandise, wore the shirts, watched the trailers, read the books, played the video games, and created an entire career around how that story inspired me. That story is a part of me.

We all have examples of stories that have been part of our lives. I watched all the seasons of *Breaking Bad,* which was over five years. I have seen every *Seinfeld* episode and all the *Curb Your Enthusiasm* episodes as well (and still re-watch them), so that is over twenty years! I watched all of *Downton Abbey* and I still am watching *The Walking Dead* and *Game of Thrones.* My wife and I usually consume a new Netflix series every month!

When I was asked to be the company historian, I needed to develop a baseline knowledge, and I spent over five years studying and learning all the key P&G brand stories along with the company history. Today I share those daily across the globe. They are now part of me, and I am still learning new stories every day!

> Pull apart the stories you like. What you like in them is part of you ... [Y]ou've got to recognize, learn, and practice those things before you can use them.[15]
>
> **—Emma Coats, PIXAR**

Learn from the stories that you like best

One secret to being a great storyteller is to learn how to dissect your favorite stories. To understand them. To understand what makes them work. Why do you love them? What do they make you feel? Why is the hero interesting? Why is the villain or problem engaging? What did you learn from the story?

You need to understand the bad ones, too. You need to understand what *not to do,* and what really makes the difference between 90 percent on Rotten Tomatoes (the movie review website that combines both professional critics' reviews and the general public's thoughts) and 12 percent. Trust me, it's not usually budget.[16]

The insights that make your favorite stories great

can also manifest themselves in your story; in fact, the answers are there right in front of you.

You just have to look, understand them, and practice.

WORKBOOK

Chapter Two Questions

Question: What stories would you share internally to best demonstrate your company's beliefs? What stories would you share to challenge and inspire a project team?

____

____

____

Question: Consider the movies or TV shows that you are watching right now. What societal insights do you see in them?

____

____

____

____

____

____

____

____

____

____

____

____

Chapter Two Notes

CHAPTER THREE

Deep Dive: What Is a Story?

It has been almost fifteen years since I read *Story* by Robert McKee, and I still have that first copy with all my notes scribbled in it right next to my desk. It was a groundbreaking piece of work and one of my favorites.

I have attended the McKee Story Seminar in New York City three different times, and each time I have found it just as riveting. One key thing McKee taught me, both in his book and at his seminar, was the importance of a storyteller being both a psychologist and an artist. As I said earlier, to be a great storyteller, you have to understand people, plain and simple. If you don't understand how people think, what they feel, and how to engage their emotional limits, then how do you expect your story to have any real power? You also need to be creative and find unique ways to bring your story to life.

McKee's seminar is full of invaluable information.

If you attend one of his seminars, you will leave with pages and pages of notes. But the idea he shared that probably changed me the most was his simple but profound definition of *story*. It became the lens through which I would look at almost every business problem. Here it is.

> Storytelling is the creative demonstration of truth, the living proof of an idea and the conversion of idea to action.[17]
>
> **—Robert McKee**

I have this committed to memory. It is a wonderful way to understand what a great story is and what it needs to do. Your brand needs to be a demonstration of the truth you believe in. It is the living proof of your beliefs, and the best brands also create an action. They bring about a transformation. How has it changed people—your audience? Do they feel different, think differently, behave differently? If your story's idea created no action, then what power did it have?

The iPhone was Steve Jobs and Apple's truth, the living proof of their idea, and think of the actions and transformations it has inspired. Think of all the ways your life has changed because of this super computer you now carry in your pocket.

That is a great story.

Great stories always start with people

Sometimes, you can even look at the people closest to you for your story inspiration.

For example, Victor Mills was a key scientist at P&G through the '40s and '50s. One day, he was changing his grandson's cloth diaper on a family vacation and thought to himself, "My gosh, there has to be a better way to do this." That insight turned out to be the beginning of what would become the Pampers disposable diaper.

Similarly, in the 1950s, a South African chemist (Graham Wulff) learned of his wife's displeasure with the night creams that were available. She said they were all too thick and oily. With her as his inspiration, he developed a radical new product that not only became a hit with her but eventually with women around the globe. It is called Olay.

And Vicks VapoRub was created by a father for his son.[18] I tell all three of those stories to P&G employees as a way to remind them that a single consumer insight can inspire a completely new product. They are also a reminder that those closest to you can also be the inspiration you may need. Many of the best *Seinfeld* episodes came from the writers' personal stories.[19]

Always start with people—what is their truth?

A word of caution before we move on: truth, or at least perception of truth, is a matter of perspective. Your truth is not everyone's truth. Truth in this sense is a point of view. With a great story, you have to understand and be conscious that what you *share* and *show* may not be what the audience *sees* and *hears*. That is why you have to understand your audience.

A lot of businesses understand finances and spreadsheets but can completely miss the "understanding people" part. Don't make that mistake. The best brands know their consumers way before they focus on a technology, financial model, or deployment strategy. Don't create a solution looking for a problem. Start with a real problem for your consumer and fix it. Be a part of their story. Know their truth.

Be that brand.

The danger of getting caught up on plot

All stories need to have a plot.

Plot is essentially *what happens*. It is a series of events. The problem is that most plots are already out there. You have already seen them. That is why the plot is not as important as the actual story. The key difference is that a story is what the characters feel and do because of *what happens*. We want to see how the plot affects people and what they feel and do because

of it.

Like I said, most plots have been done before in some way. In fact, you should Google the video "Everything is a Remix" by Kirby Ferguson. Everyone from Shakespeare to modern-day directors have been reimagining, leveraging, and remixing storylines that have come before them.[20]

Story may be what the human race does best. Think about it. What do you really do that isn't story related? Trends start with stories. Wars start over stories. Companies and brands start with a story. People create, protect, and share stories. I can't think of a truly significant human innovation that didn't start with a story. Stories get mashed together with other stories, and new ones are created.

Many technologies started from stories

Have you ever realized how much story has influenced technological change? In his book *The Storytelling Animal*, Jonathan Gottschall writes:

> The more deeply we are cast under the story's spell, the more potent the influence. In fact, fiction is more potent at challenging belief than nonfiction.[21]
>
> **—Jonathan Gottschall**

Science fiction has changed the world. Martin Cooper, inventor of the cell phone, was inspired by

Captain Kirk's communicator. The film *Minority Report* got the tech community excited about the idea of facial recognition, predictive crime fighting, and driverless cars. Tony Stark's CAD system from the movie *Iron Man* inspired Elon Musk to create a gesture-based CAD system (which you can watch him use on YouTube).[22] In 1926, Robert Goddard, one of the pioneers of the rocket, wanted to go to space because he had read the H. G. Wells book *War of the Worlds*. Simon Lake, one of the key creators of the submarine, was inspired by Jules Verne's book *20,000 Leagues Under the Sea*.[23]

Science fiction has always pushed the imagination of scientists and engineers around the world.

But you have to be careful with technology. Technology has no meaning or purpose without people who want to learn and use it. A Ridley Scott quote (one of my favorite directors and filmmakers) about technology says it all:

> You might do a magnificent job of creating an unfamiliar world—a far place, a far-off time, or both—with the most skilled filmmakers and the best technology available. But you have to make sure that world is inhabited by people whose lives and fates we care about and whose story has something to say to us.[24]
>
> **—Ridley Scott**

To put that quote into business world terms, remember that just because you have a great technology does not mean you have a great story. How does it affect people?

Focusing on technology alone is not enough anymore

You have to deeply understand and know your *who* and *why* before you focus on the *what*. Who is your technology for? Why do they need it? And how will it help them?

Having great technology is honestly not that difficult today. When was the last time you went into a Best Buy, saw a TV, and were appalled by its poor resolution? Having great technology today is just the new point of entry, regardless of the category. It is simply a minimum to proceed. Great technology alone will no longer be enough to differentiate you. You will need a great story to go along with it.

Heck, even Intel doesn't talk much about speed anymore, I would guess because all computers are pretty fast these days and the average consumer can no longer tell the difference. Instead, Intel seems to be sharing a lot more about what they are working on to change the future.

So, what story would you tell to show how your technology is raising the bar and changing people's lives?

Remember, incremental change does not necessarily equal innovation. Inside a company's walls, it can be easy to confuse what is perhaps revolutionary for your company versus the industry at large. Don't make that mistake. You have to see and understand the bigger story.

Technology should only help tell the story

You should always have a great story to go with great technology. It's not just what people buy anymore—it's what they buy into.

Same goes for a movie.

A product's technology is the same as a movie's special effects. The effects (the technology) are there to help bring the story to life.

There are two different types of movies: ones that make the special effects the story, and ones that use the special effects to help tell the bigger story.

You want to be the latter.

You can always tell when there wasn't much story and the hope was to distract the audience with a variety of explosions or CG effects. In his widely referenced work *The Poetics*, Aristotle said that the best stories leverage spectacle last.[25] The primary focus should always be on the story, the characters, the dialogue, and the meaning. The spectacle (technology) is only there to support the story.

You don't make 4K resolution the story; you

make how it will change consumers' lives the story. Or maybe you focus on the brand's reputation in innovation, its heritage, or its commitment to quality as the story.

But make no mistake: someone will offer whatever your "4K" is very soon, and it will be just as good, if not better, than what you're currently offering. That is why you seldom see a movie with bad effects anymore.

Having good technology isn't what creates a great story; it's what you are doing uniquely with it that will set you apart.

The technology world is shifting exponentially

Peter Diamandis offers an inspiring (and a bit scary) presentation in his book *Bold*, which shows us how exponentially fast innovation is occurring. Many companies will be left behind if they can't be amazingly agile and willing to alter their traditional thinking, completely reframing their business model in some cases.

Diamandis talks about having an "abundance mindset." We are in a world where technology is shifting to one of abundance, not scarcity. If your technology lives off of scarcity, you need to realize that someone is trying to make it abundant, and if they do they will completely change, if not destroy, your business model.

That is potentially every company's Achilles' heel. What does your company protect that, if it were easy to get or cheap to make, would effectively end your brand? Think about making information accessible anywhere (Google), using your car as a taxi (Uber), or opening rooms in your house as a hotel (Airbnb).

Traditional taxis, hotels, and libraries had limited access by requiring special permits, brick and mortar buildings, limited quantities, etc. They had to evolve their story. The lesson? Companies with a scarcity mindset could potentially find themselves looking more like the story of the dodo—extinct.

If you could synthesize gold for $1 an ounce, how valuable would conventionally mined and refined gold become on the retail market? Once something becomes cheap and abundant, its previous value quickly diminishes. And, at that point, you better own a different part of the business model. For example, maybe your company would need to own the machines that manufacture the gold.

The story in business will continue to change, with or without you. Agility means something very different today than it did just ten years ago.

It's always better to be the one changing the story than waiting to be a victim of it.[26]

What brand story are you telling the world?

What story would get me excited about your company or your products? Have you ever thought about what might revolutionize, or perhaps destroy, your industry?

Here is an interesting exercise I do with project teams that I suggest you try as well:

Write a newspaper story about the end of your company and what caused it—essentially an obituary of your company, product, or brand. Headlines and all.

I did that once for a management team meeting over ten years ago, and there are still people who talk about it today. With a little cutting and pasting, you can raise some serious eyebrows. It's a great way to use story to spark an idea, get people thinking, incite action, or share a point of view.

There are so many different types of stories you can create in the business world. But at the end of the day you really have a choice between two. You can create:

> A timeless classic that touches heart and soul and sets the bar for the next generation and makes money.

Or

> A story that makes money but feels formulaic and is devoid of originality.

It seems like a simple decision, but how many of the first are there in comparison to the second?

Notice how I said *both* make money. Making money is no sign of a great story. There are plenty of very bad stories, products, and brands that make money. Money doesn't mean they'll be timeless classics that touch the heart and soul. It doesn't mean they will inspire others.

Let me ask you this: Do you want your next brand idea to be more like *The Godfather Part II* or *Paul Blart: Mall Cop II*? (*Godfather II* has a 97 percent approval rating on Rotten Tomatoes, and *Paul Blart II* has a 5 percent rating.) One of those is a timeless story, studied and shown year after year, and has set a new bar for filmmakers while cementing itself as part of the AFI (American Film Institute) Top 100. A true classic. The other is a way to get a quick laugh on a Saturday afternoon, but don't expect much more than that.

Now, don't get me wrong. I enjoy a good laugh or special effects spectacle from time to time. But they don't really stick with me the same way *The Godfather* does, nor do they make me think or feel something powerful, like Peter Jackson's *Lord of the Rings* films.

What story do you want to leave behind?

A leader at P&G once said that "culture is the stories that people tell when management is not in the room."[27]

What do you want the stories about *you* to be when you're not in the room? What stories do you want to be known for? What legacy do you want to leave behind?

Being a historian is also being part anthropologist. As the P&G company historian, I do many employee interviews to not only capture the institutional knowledge but to also get the pulse of the company at that moment in time. For example, one of the questions I ask people who are retiring is, "If you could leave behind just one story for future generations to learn and be inspired from, what story would it be?" It's a hard question, because it limits them to only one. One story for people to look back on. One story to capture their most valuable insight and lesson.

If you were asked that today, what would yours be?

In the end, I let them tell as many stories as they want, but I always start with that question to really get them thinking.

WORKBOOK

Chapter Three Questions

Question: What would be the first few sentences of your brand's "sci-fi story"? What does the future look like?

____

____

____

____

____

____

____

____

____

____

Question: What would be the title and first few sentences of your company's "obituary story"? What would make your brand obsolete? What is your Achilles' heel?

Chapter Three Notes

CHAPTER FOUR

Stories Create Action

Stories are like an internal operating system that guides how you think, how you learn, how you get inspired, and most importantly, how you see other people.

Humans are a collective story repository, passing our stories from one generation to the next. Stories are literally a generational memory. Every hero needs to be regularly inspired as he or she moves through the chapters of life. No matter what ideas or activities rev you up, I'm sure there is a story behind them.

Stories, and the desire to be a part of them, drive a lot of human behavior. The power of a story helps motivate you to accept that job offer and see a bright future, ask that girl or guy to marry you, choose that career and dedicate your life to it, be a leader in that club or organization, and pick up the phone and call a friend to see if they want to go see the new *Star Wars* movie.

Great stories not only make you take action—they also affect the actions of others.

How your heroes affect you

I have a passion for history, and it has always been something I enjoy reading and learning about. Where did that interest come from? I have had many influences, but two really stick out. One is a fictional character named Indiana Jones, and the other was my high school history teacher, Mr. Sowards.

What I loved about Mr. Sowards was that he rarely used a textbook in class; instead, he told stories about the characters and moments of history. He would immerse us into history by putting us right in the shoes of different historical figures and asking what we'd do in their situation. He was forcing us to learn the idea of empathy, wanting us to see what they may have seen and feel what they may have felt.

Empathy is critical for a good story. You have to be able to feel with the heroes and understand why they made the choices they did because, again, it is their truth.

Your company can provide a consumer with all the data and facts in the world, but those will in no way guarantee trust or belief. With empathy you need to focus on the "why," not necessarily the "how."

For example, it is like thinking about the same story but from different points of view. Like the conquered and the conquering, the attackers and the defenders, the hero and the anti-hero. Each of those perspectives has vastly different stories from the same moment in time and during the exact same conflict. Coincidentally, they are all "true" as well. Mr. Sowards helped me understand that.

When I tell the P&G company history, I don't just talk chronology and present the dates. Those aren't as important as being able to understand and share the key themes, insights, changes, and lessons from the past. Those help show and explain why P&G did what they did and how those actions led to many great innovations and brands.

P&G's goal is to touch and improve lives, and every story in our archives is there to help demonstrate and share that.

Indiana Jones also got me excited about history.

After watching *Raiders of the Lost Ark,* I developed a keen interest in archeology. I must have read a dozen books on that subject after seeing the film. There was something so fascinating about looking back through history and piecing together different parts of the story. It is detective work. Now I do that as my full-time job.

Both Mr. Sowards and Indiana Jones's stories inspired me to take action. To do what I really love.

Batman is another one of my heroes. He had no

special powers other than his wit, determination, and ingenuity. I loved that about him, and it always reminded me that even I could maybe be a superhero.

One of the houses I grew up in, a neat old house outside of Columbus, Ohio, had its very own "Bat Cave" (it was really a root cellar). My dad rigged up a little Bat Computer for me using old electronics; my mom created a detective chemistry set with some jars, water, and food coloring. She also made me the coolest homemade Batman outfit any kid could hope for. Those root cellar doors were my gateway to fighting the underbelly of Gotham every day. So much of my ingenuity and creative spirit came from thinking like Batman as a kid. I had empathy for him and could put myself in his shoes.

I honestly have a long list of heroes who have helped me—examples that range from family to fantasy, from my grandpa to Luke Skywalker.

Remember, you are a product of the stories you hold most dear. Who are your heroes? You can learn a lot about someone when you ask them that. Do that with your team. Have each person share who their heroes are and how they influenced them.

Who are your company's heroes? Once you know and understand those, it can help better clarify your purpose—what your company is really trying to do and how it does it.

WORKBOOK

Chapter Four Questions

Question: Who are five of your heroes, and how have they changed who you are?

___

___

___

___

___

___

___

___

___

___

___

Question: What is your company's purpose? What heroes would your company hold up as a representation of that purpose, and how are those stories shared?

Chapter Four Notes

CHAPTER FIVE

Stories Make People Care

There are only two types of stories out there: good and bad.

You can use all kinds of fancy nomenclature for your stories, like product story, brand story, consumer story, culture story, company story, or technology story. But in the end, it's simply either good or bad. The kind of story we remember, or the kind of story we forget.

Good stories stick. They're retold because they create an emotional link within you.

How can you use a story to demonstrate a company's culture? Let me share one of my favorites. At the end of the book, I will share an example of how a bad culture story can be just as powerful.

Steve is a friend I worked with at P&G for almost twenty years. One day, Steve and I were catching up over a cup of coffee and ended up sharing our "first time taking kids to Disney World" stories. Disney World's culture is legendary when it comes to understanding their guests, and Steve's story quickly became one of my favorite examples to share.

Steve, his wife, and their two daughters were all thrilled about going to Disney World. It was their first time as a family.

Their day started at "The Crystal Palace" (a very popular breakfast restaurant in the Magic Kingdom) at an event called the "Winnie the Pooh Breakfast Buffet." While waiting for the characters to make their way to their table, Steve's youngest (just seven years old) had gone up to the breakfast buffet to get some food. Bringing back her plate of eggs, potatoes, and bacon, she decided to start with the potatoes and grabbed the ketchup bottle. As she began to squirt the ketchup onto her plate, it sputtered and burped—almost empty. She tapped it against the table but it still didn't work.

Then she began to shake it vigorously toward the plate. That got the ketchup out, but not the way she wanted.

The air pocket blocking the ketchup gave way, and a burst of ketchup exploded from the bottle, all over her shirt! A meltdown quickly followed, and tears streamed down her face. But she was not upset about her shirt or the ketchup. Instead, with tears dripping, she told her mom and dad that she was sorry because now she would ruin all the pictures that day with her stained shirt.

Mom and dad comforted her immediately and asked her what she wanted to do. She said she wanted to go back to the resort to get a change of clothes.

They decided the best solution was going to be to split up. Steve would take her back to the resort while mom and their other daughter would stay in the park and start riding. They would simply meet up later. But understand, a trip back to a resort during peak season to get a change of clothes is not a short one.

So here they were, a couple of hours into their first day on their first trip to Disney World, and they already were going to have to split up.

Enter the magic that is Disney.

Before he left, his wife said she would take their daughter to the bathroom and get as much of the ketchup off as she could. While they were in there, the janitor walked in. The janitor immediately saw the teary eyed little girl, knelt down, and asked her what had happened.

After hearing her story, the janitor told her not to worry and that her day would be wonderful. She also told her that they shouldn't have to split up. This was their first trip there, after all, and they should have every moment together as a family.

The janitor got up, said that she would be right

back, and left the bathroom. Within a flash, she returned and told their daughter to have a magical day and to enjoy being there with her family, handing over a gift card for her to get a new shirt, anywhere in the park, no limit.

The day was saved!

More than that, an incredible memory and story was created with something as simple as a gift card—a truly "magical moment." The shirt purchased that day is still part of the family's scrapbook. They even have a picture of the janitor with their youngest. For many summers after that, both their daughters would ask, "When are we going back to Disney World?"

When I share this story at events, it's not uncommon for people in the audience to come up afterward and share their own Disney magic stories. I have heard tons of them. I even have many stories myself (I will share some later).

Disney understands the power of a great memory and the incredible role a story plays.

But here is the big question: What is a janitor paid to do? To clean. But, what does a Disney janitor love to do? To create magic moments for guests like every other employee at Disney, regardless of rank or title.

All Disney employees are asked to create magic moments for their guests each and every day, and each Disney employee is empowered to do that.

With that idea in mind, what are you paid to do? I don't want a general job description based on your degree or title. Anyone can do that. I want to hear a story that would show how much you love what you do. I want to hear a story that would demonstrate your passion for what you do. That is what great stories are made of.

Disney is a company that clearly understands a very simple story principle, and it is this:

- Emotions influence decisions.
- Stories influence emotions.
- Therefore, stories have a great deal of power.

A good story is one that captures emotion and inspires action. A good story will make me care. If you can't make me care, I won't. Be clear on what you want people to really care about.

So, which story is yours—good or bad?

WORKBOOK

Chapter Five Questions

Question: What is one of your company's best culture stories—one that really demonstrates your purpose and why your employees love what they do?

___

___

Question: What story would you share with your team at the beginning of a project to truly make them care about what they are working on?

___

___

___

___

___

___

___

___

___

___

___

___

Chapter Five Notes

CHAPTER SIX

Stories Can Change the World

> Stories have power. They delight, enchant, touch, teach, recall, inspire, motivate, and challenge. They help us understand. They imprint a picture on our minds. ... Want to make a point or raise an issue? Tell a story.[28]
>
> **—Janet Litherland**

Stories are one of the best ways to create change, show why it's needed, or get support behind it.

Not long ago, I was asked to speak about the world of story at a company women's network meeting. Given my passion for movies, I decided to create a presentation on "The Changing World of Women in Film." It was an area I was interested in and had recently read some articles on, but I needed to do more research before my talk.

This is an area that needs some *big* change. According to one statistic I found, women directed only around 4.7 percent of the major studio movies released from 2011 to 2016.[29]

Back in 1979, TV director Victoria Hochberg and five other female directors found that only 0.5 percent of all the job assignments in both TV and film were going to women.[30] Progress is being made to double the number of women in film by 2020,[31] but there is still a lot of work to do.

There are other big problem areas, too, like ageism, ridiculous beauty standards, and the number of speaking parts given to men versus women.

Did you know that as recently as 2014, only 12 percent of movie lead protagonists were female? That same year, only 30 percent of speaking characters were female.[32]

Well-known American actress, film producer, and writer Geena Davis is doing a lot of work to bring equality to women in film and recently worked with the University of Southern California (USC) and Google to create the Geena Davis Inclusion Quotient (GD-IQ).[33]

GD-IQ is a software that scans films in rapid time and measures the quantity and quality of dialogue between men and women. When studying the 100 top-grossing films of 2015, she and her team found:[34]

- Male characters had nearly twice the scene and speaking time.
- Male leads spoke three times as often as the female characters in the film, but female leads had similar speaking time to the male characters.
- In action films, males had nearly three times the scene and speaking time, even though films with lead female protagonists gross 15.8 percent more on average than films with a male lead.

This is just a quick snapshot of what I found with online searches. But what does it all really mean?

It means that what people see on the screen matters, and we need to be more conscious of that.

Where do you think a lot of young girls see portrayals of women in society? In the media! Here's what Geena Davis has to say:

> For every one female character, there are three male characters. ... The reason I focused on what happens in front of the camera is because I feel we are training people from the very beginning, from when they're a little toddler, to see women as less important and less competent. We're not seeing women in leadership positions, so therefore, we're not seeing it in real life.
>
> On TV, there are so many female forensic scientists, because of CSI and those shows, that colleges are scrambling to keep up with the number of women who want to study forensic science because they've

> seen it and they say, "Hey, that looks great. I could do that."
>
> ...If they see it, they can be it.[35]

"If they see it, they can be it." I love that, and it really makes clear why change is needed. The Director of *Kung Fu Panda II*, Jennifer Yuh Nelson, said this:

> I don't think about the gender thing much. But when I speak at schools, I've had female students say to me afterwards, "I never envisioned myself being a director, since I've never seen women do it." But after seeing me, they can picture themselves directing...[36]

Changing the traditional protagonist

The good news is that movies are starting to change the roles of women, both in front of and behind the camera. Finally, the traditional damsel in distress stereotype is disappearing. Many female protagonists have had major influences through characters like Princess Leia, Ellen Ripley, Thelma & Louise, Norma Rae, Hermione Granger, and Katniss Everdeen.

Recently, another strong female character named Rey represented another fresh take on female characters in film.

In *Star Wars: The Force Awakens*, Rey is the main

hero, and she is a strong, independent, courageous, and compassionate character. She doesn't need to be saved—she is there to help do the saving, a force of her own to be reckoned with. But the biggest thing that Rey may accomplish is to change how boys think of girls.

Rey absolutely is a role model for girls, but she may be an even more powerful role model for boys. Girls already know they are tough. It's boys who need to see and hear that message.

Rey will be a role model for the next generation of boys and girls playing *Star Wars* on the playgrounds and in the schoolyards. She has shown boys what women can do. Over the last several years, we've seen the end of what many call the old "someday my Prince will come" storyline. Progress is being made.

The message of *Star Wars: The Force Awakens* immediately reminded me of another great story from the feminine hygiene brand Always: the #LikeAGirl campaign.

First aired during the 2015 Super Bowl, it is helping change how society talks about what girls do.

> Yes, women can always use more strong women role models in popular culture but ... we didn't need to know we "could" do all the things men can. We just needed the rest of the world to know it, too.[37]
>
> —**Alecia Morgan, *Huffington Post***

For the 2017 International Women's Day, I noticed iTunes reorganized its movie purchase page into subjects titled Direct "Like A Girl," Write "Like a Girl," Act "Like A Girl," Fight "Like A Girl," and Laugh "Like A Girl." That is the role a great story can play.

Stories can shift thought, alter society, and plant the seeds for needed change. We hear about new movements every day and they all start with sharing a powerful story.

Stories produce genuine recall

One of my favorite lines from the film *Fight Club* is when Tyler Durden (played by Brad Pitt) says: "The things you own end up owning you."[38]

Great stories have lines that can make you look at life differently. Think about all the lines from film that you know, use, and hear outside of the theater. Many of them have simply become part of society, just like "There is no place like home" from *The Wizard of Oz*.[39] You not only can recall those lines, but you know and understand why.

I sometimes hear businesses ask, "How was the recall for that ad?" That is kind of a silly question, because "recall" does not necessarily have a direct link with a positive passion. I can recall many things that I have no further desire to ever see or try again. It has to be "recalled" for the right reason and with the right emotion.

One of my old bosses in P&G Design said something to me years ago that I will never forget. He said, "Shane, a two-headed dog is distinctive, but that doesn't mean I want one." Just because you stand out does not mean you have a good story. Just because people "recall" your ad doesn't mean it was any good. Just because you can "yell loud" doesn't mean you actually have anything worth saying.

Trying to stand out without a great story usually creates an empty promise and an inauthentic experience that can make consumers resentful.

Remember what happened to little Ralphie and his treasured decoder ring in the classic movie *A Christmas Story?* He was bamboozled, tricked, and misdirected. He thought there was a real story, when in fact it was just a "crummy commercial" (his words).[40]

The world of advertising could learn a lot from that movie. The answer has been sitting in front of them all this time with a timeless holiday film that I'm sure most of them watch every year.

And yet, how many crummy commercials are there? How many are trying too hard to just sell me something? That are more concerned with inspiring a purchase than making a connection?

Keith Reinhard (advertising guru, Advertising Hall of Fame member, and chairman emeritus of DDB Worldwide) said there is a big difference between creating buzz and creating a brand.

> There's an important difference between a one-off stunt and an enduring brand story. There's a difference between an algorithm and an insight into human nature and between mere contact and true connection. Finally, there's a wide gulf between big data and a big idea.[41]

Stories can engage people through emotions

There is an old Native American proverb that says, "Those who tell the stories rule the world."

Do you realize how much time you spend each year just to be entertained? To laugh, cry, and feel fear and excitement? Don't just think TV or movies. Think your hobbies, conferences, TED Talks, YouTube, video games, books, magazines, websites and the internet, shopping, museums, theme parks, vacations, or just an evening out at a restaurant. We love to be entertained! And stories do that better than anything.

Entertainment is engagement, and engagement leads to emotion.

Once you are engaged, it's much easier to learn. Unfortunately, the educational system sometimes still struggles with this. Too much teaching still uses antiquated models of providing content with the objective of passing short-term goals (quizzes and tests).

Remember when you were in college and you

took those first couple years of classes, the general education ones—classes such as economics 101, sociology 101, art history 101, etc.? Do you remember the content from those classes? As you studied for those classes, why weren't you thinking to yourself, "Wow, this is great information—I'm so glad I am learning this!"

You probably didn't say that, and here is why: in most cases, the education system has said that the success benchmark for learning is to get past scheduled tests and due dates, and not necessarily to show the content's application in your daily life.

A lot of general education is about short-term memorization instead of long-term understanding. If you don't find relevance or use for something, where will your brain most likely put it? Answer: either in short-term memory or the mental trash bin. After cramming the night before for a test, memorizing all of the necessary content, you end up opening a little valve in your head afterwards and it all floats away. That is usually not the content's fault, but instead how it was presented.

Now ask yourself this: is information you care about easier to remember? Does it stick? If the information triggers some kind of emotion, does it become more memorable? If you can't feel it, you probably won't remember it! I'd bet that the more degree-specific courses you took in college are much easier to remember. Why? Because you could see how they would eventually affect your day-today life. They felt more important! They were presented with direct relevance to what you would be doing to make your living. You were able to understand why you needed them.

How a story is delivered plays an important role. We simply have no time for content that we don't see as valuable.

But a story that is told well can help us see value in almost anything.

One of my other favorite teachers never used a "memorize this" mindset. His name was Mr. Sanchez, and he was my second grade teacher. He did this wonderful thing of teaching math through a "story problem." Whenever class started and it was math time, the students came alive with excitement because we knew that meant story time. Think about that for a second...

Math time equaled story time!

I don't know about you, but I know several writers and math whizzes who'd squirm at the thought of mixing the two! At least at first. But if they saw Mr. Sanchez at work, they'd understand the power of what he was doing in a heartbeat.

Mr. Sanchez used a small jungle picture backdrop for his math problems, and, upon our urging, often plucked animals out of a tackle box to help him illustrate whatever problem we were working on. He would ask, "Okay, what animals are in our story today?"

"Crocodiles!" we'd yell, and he'd withdraw a

couple of crocs from the box and place them in the river on his jungle diorama.

"What else?"

"Zebras!" we'd yell. Then he would take out maybe five of those.

Then came the story.

He would paint the scene, show the zebras approach the river, and then ask us what happens next.

"Each crocodile eats a zebra!"

He made that happen, and then asked, "So, how many are left that ran away?"

Quickly counting, someone would say, "Three got away."

We could see math helping us understand what was around us, whether cars in a parking lot, pencils on a desk, or French fries on our plate. It had nothing to do with Arabic numerals—he simply made math real and relevant to our day to day. He made it a visual story.

Years later, I found out that he was way ahead of his time, as there is now a method called Singapore Math making its way across the US and other parts of the world since the Nineties. It operates with a similar vision: that math is all about using visual storytelling to explain how it works. Singapore Math focuses on the *how*, not just the *why*. Using story principles, it bridges the concrete and the abstract:

Since the Trends in International Mathematics and Science Study started ranking countries' competitiveness in math literacy in 1995, Singapore has consistently ranked among the best. Established by the International Association for the Evaluation of Educational Achievement, TIMSS 2011, the most recent report, ranked Singaporean fourth-graders in first place and eighth-graders in second.

Another international study, the Program for International Student Assessment, shows Singapore's fifteen-year-olds are among the best at problem-solving and are able to solve unstructured problems in unfamiliar contexts.

As a doctoral student at Northeastern University, Kevin Mahoney, a math coordinator at a school near Boston, published the first study examining the effects of Singaporean teaching techniques on American students.

"Across the board in every case, all of these students were able to make substantial gains," Mahoney said.

"In the States, we tend to—whether we like it or not—we believe children are born with mathematical ability," Mahoney said. "But that's not true in countries like Singapore, where it's believed that effort is the thing that makes you smarter in math."[42]

Singapore Math is about mastery, not memorization. Ten thousand hours of visual stories, *not* ten thousand hours of cramming for tests.

Stories can move people to action

Think about the lessons and memories from some of your favorite movies. I still get teary-eyed every time I watch the scene in *Toy Story 3* where Andy gives his toys to the little girl. I have been there before, we all have—the moment we realized we weren't kids anymore. The *Toy Story* series is about Andy's journey from childhood to adulthood.

I still feel like starting a new exercise regimen when I watch *300* and its representation of the Battle of Thermopylae. The same with *Rocky*: you see him training to that classic soundtrack and tell yourself that maybe it's time to start jogging again.

I still feel uneasy when I hear the haunting soundtrack of *Jaws*. I would be lying if I said it didn't come into my head when I visit the beach and swim in the ocean.

Excitement, fear, love, happiness, passion all show up in daily life too—in careers, at home, with your friends and family. Your brain doesn't care if it is a movie, book, or family story. Emotion is emotion.

And emotion is everything.

Watch this video on YouTube by Purple Feather (an agency in the UK). Just Google, "It's a beautiful day and I can't see it." It opens with a blind man sitting on the street, asking for change. His sign reads: "I am blind, please help." People keep walking by, but little money drops into his cup.

Partway through the video, a woman stops, picks up his sign, turns it over, and writes something. She walks off and, for the next several minutes, people start to put change in his cup. Lots of it!

It isn't until the end that we can see what she wrote: "It is a beautiful day and I can't see it."[43]

Fantastic!

This is a person who understands that a story has to be told with empathy. If the audience can't or doesn't empathize with the hero, then the story fails. The statement she wrote puts the story into the passerby's point of view. The only person who can know it is a beautiful day is someone who can see. The statement changed it from the blind man's perspective to the audience's perspective so they could better understand what he had to deal with every day of his life.

Here's another example. One day online, I stumbled upon an experiment in hitchhiking. Someone was testing different signs. Could a change in a few words make people more likely to stop? The first sign said something like, "Columbus, Ohio." That one doesn't really do much, does it? The second sign was "Mom's for Christmas." Now that has a relatable story! If someone stops for that, the first question they will have to ask is, "so, where is Mom's?" Then the hitchhiker can say "Columbus."

Emotion in a story becomes the hook people need. Have a lot of data in your presentation? Fine, but you need to get people's hearts involved first. Start with emotion and then get into the data. It has to be head *and* heart, not head *or* heart (we will talk more about this later).

Stories that touch the heart have widespread impact. Have you seen the dead raccoon story from Toronto? Just Google it! It's one of my favorites! I've shared it probably two hundred times from Amsterdam to Australia, and there is always someone in the audience who has seen it. That is the power and virality of clever stories today.

Basically, what you have is a guy in Toronto boarding his usual city bus one morning and he notices a dead raccoon right by the stop. He uses his iPhone, along with social media, to let the city know. They respond quickly and tell him that they had already been notified and were taking care of it.

Problem solved, right?

Not quite.

As the day went on, the city didn't clean up the raccoon quick enough, and people decided to draw attention to that by telling a story. A very funny one. Someone brought a framed picture of a raccoon and set it by the spot. Flowers were dropped off, signed cards placed nearby—it even got its own hashtag, #DeadRaccoonTO!

Night fell and it still sat on the sidewalk by the bus stop. Candles were brought and placed around the raccoon. Someone even took a picture of their trash bin and asked people to leave their bins open that night in honor of the raccoon. Dozens upon dozens of pictures spanned the internet soon thereafter.

Then finally the next day, hours and hours later, the city arrived and cleaned up the raccoon.

After that, someone came and painted one of those murder scene outlines on the sidewalk!

Why did all of this happen? What was this *really* about? A raccoon?

No. It was about how slow many residents felt the city was. The raccoon became a character in a story to draw attention to the time it took to get a bus stop cleaned up.[44]

Always ask yourself what your story is *really* about. More importantly, ask yourself what you want your story to do. There are many clever ways to bring it to life, but start with the meaning and the action you want people to take.

Your stories have the power to change the world.

WORKBOOK

Chapter Six Questions

Question: How do you use a story to teach or inspire at work?

Question: What stories made you think differently about an issue? Why did they work?

Chapter Six Notes

CHAPTER SEVEN

The Unique Insight in a Story

Great stories start with an insight, and the best insights usually come from good ol' fashioned research and observation. You need to understand your subjects and characters deeply (the same goes for developing a strong brand story). You have to get into their life.

Doing a couple of focus groups isn't enough. You have to dig deep and know your material inside and out.

Let's say you wanted to create a story about gangsters and the mob and your "research" consists of watching a couple of movies on the topic. That's not going to make you an expert, and you'll probably just end up creating clichéd scenes.

You need to find unique insights, and you only find those through lots of different types of research: interviews, books, media, oral histories, observation—maybe even being a part of the group you are studying. As your knowledge base grows, you learn to read between the lines, which is often where unique insight lives. Know your hero and your audience. In the end, it can't be your story; it has to become theirs!

It's the same with brands. You cannot always rely on consumers to explain exactly what they want. In many cases, what people say and what they do are very different.

People usually don't look for change, but that doesn't mean they don't want it—and that's where you come in. I used to have a five-disc carousel player and CD tower and couldn't imagine my music system ever getting better. Now I don't know what I'd do without my digital collection and my portable Bluetooth speaker! What's next?

How do you find unique insights?

Back in the 90s, a Mr. Clean formulator was doing an in-home visit with a woman to watch her mop and ask questions about one of their new formulas. While discussing the product, the consumer told the formulator that all of the Mr. Clean formulas worked great—but there was a problem.

She walked over to her broom closet, opened it, and revealed the problem: all of the stuff required to mop her floor.

Buckets. Mops. Special tools. She told him to fix *that*.

This story was the catalyst for a project that later became the Swiffer WetJet.[45] It's a great P&G example of finding the insight.

Think about it. All it took was one person to eventually affect hundreds of thousands and redefine a category.

A word of caution on "focus groups": great insights can be tough to find there. Focus groups may be *ok* for quick reactions to ideas, but don't expect deep insights! Why? Because focus groups are one step from being an SAT test: a bland room full of tables with a moderator and a hidden audience full of strangers watching you. Pencils down, time's up!

Does that sound like a normal environment where products get used?

Not even close.

Unique insights come from things like one-on-ones, in-home visits, and shop-a-longs. You have to watch people use a product. They come from listening as much as talking. You have to go to the place where the product or brand is being used. You have to watch people very closely and learn from them.

P&G understands this. It's why the company shows and tests its products in the environment in which they will be used. If you are creating a new dish soap, then talking about it in a focus group room doesn't make much sense, because there are no sinks or dishes there!

This is the same reason you can't depend on surveys. They are impersonal, and you can't see whom you are talking to. You have to be with them. When you are talking one-on-one, you get at the issues and understand what's working and what isn't. You can probe deeper. Let the conversation roam. Study people's eyes and watch their body language.

More than ever before, consumers have tremendous influence over a brand's story—and rightfully so! After all, we can now watch all of our favorite TV shows without viewing a single commercial. It's incredible and—let's be honest—wonderful!

All consumers are now highly influential reporters and journalists because of those wonderful smartphone devices and a tool called social media. Those things have empowered everyone to be brand storytellers, and they can create either incredible good or amazing bad for your brand.

You need to provide powerful and inspiring story material for people to want and share. You need them to become part of your brand's story team.

That means you have to listen to them, know what inspires them, show them you care. In today's world, a brand's strength should be measured by how clearly your consumer can tell your story to his or her entire network.

Do you know what your audience wants?

A lot of advertising fails because companies don't understand their audience. In 2016, Marc

Pritchard (chief marketing officer of Procter & Gamble) spoke out against "poor advertising," calling the majority of it "crap." In an article by Barrett J. Brunsman of the *Cincinnati Business Courier*, Pritchard said the following:

> When we're at our best, we paint a brand masterpiece, clearing the highest bar of creative brilliance, but too often we produce crap....We found that in our quest to do dynamic, real-time marketing in the digital age we were literally producing thousands of new ads every year—with thousands of agencies and millions of media-plan changes...We thought that the best way to cut through the clutter in the digital age was to create more ads and change them constantly...We eventually concluded that as the world was getting louder, we were just adding to the noise. So we decided to stop the noise. We've made a choice to raise the bar on creativity because the consumers we serve around the world deserve our very best.[46]
>
> **—Marc Pritchard**

Are you starting to see why the Skip Ad button was created? You got it: a lot of really poor material along with antiquated, formulaic, and clichéd storylines.

In one year, P&G's commercials netted twenty-one Cannes Lions. That is walking the talk.

If anyone in your company does not feel that advertising will change significantly, and even irreversibly, over the next several years, then they are in denial.

It's not the death of advertising, just the death of how it was traditionally approached, which was normally quantity over quality.

Skip Ad wasn't created because consumers wanted to avoid ads all together but because they wanted more control and are demanding that better stories be created!

When a new trend, product, or idea emerges, companies have two choices: understand it or fight it. If they fight it, it's usually because they don't see the real story.

When Napster launched, I thought it was a really cool idea. There was something so rebellious about it. At the time, music was controlled by portable cassette and CD players. Those were great products and represented a top-of-the-line experience for taking music with you wherever you went.

Many companies fought the idea of Napster. Rather than understand the *why,* they focused on the *what* and the *how* and inevitably missed the real insight.

How are your portable cassette and CD players doing these days?

Extinct like the dinosaur.

But another company was watching all this happen, one not even in the music business. This company asked the *why* and realized there was something out of balance in the music world—an itch that Napster had started to scratch. That itch was the ability to get just one song at a time while simultaneously storing much more than eight to fifteen songs at a time.

Remember when we bought tapes or CDs for a single song? We'd shell out $15 for a CD hoping that some of the other songs were good too. But that didn't happen often. I mean, where do you think the term *one-hit wonder* came from?

Creating a mixtape became a popular activity, but it was a lot of work to make. All the back and forth between tape decks, planning out the right order, editing out DJs who would not shut up, deciding on the title for a particular mixed tape—it took hours and enormous patience.

But a computer company called Apple understood the *why* behind what consumers wanted.

Apple took their insights and created a new, legal music system that revolutionized music forever.

With the iPod and iTunes, people everywhere suddenly had "1,000 songs in your pocket."[47] Not a measly eight, twelve, or fifteen on something as fragile as a cassette tape or an easily scratched and often skip-prone CD. You were finally allowed to pick just the songs you wanted and organize them simply and easily in playlists without ever setting foot in a physical music store.

Isn't it amazing what can happen when a business adapts to the story that best meets the needs of consumers?

Be the one controlling how your story changes

I was recently at a technology conference in Silicon Valley. One of the speakers shared how Kodak had actually invented the digital camera years before any other company launched one. But the company's management pushed it away because they feared it would hurt their film business.

In essence, they forgot the real business they were in: capturing and preserving memories, *not* film and chemicals. And because they didn't see that, they filed for bankruptcy in 2012.[48]

Let me ask you this: would you rather be the one controlling how your story is changing, or a victim of it? Anyone leading a *category* has a target on their back, so you best be the one leading the *change*. It's like the old saying, evolve or die.

If you don't change, someone will.

When P&G launched Tide in 1946, the print ads

stated, "Tide cleans better than any soap made."[49] Guess who the soap market leader was in 1946?

P&G!

In other words, they knew that Tide and synthetic detergent science was the future of meeting the consumers' need for clean, fresh, bright clothes. They knew that it was better than using soap.

P&G supported the move to Tide even though it meant losing their leading soap brands, some with decades of equity behind them. Within ten years, traditional laundry soaps were essentially gone.

The Storyteller's Promise

Stories take time, period.

Years ago, I created something called the **Storyteller's Promise**. It is a guiding philosophy I tell myself before every presentation, keynote, or workshop. It reminds me that the audience is giving me one of their most valuable assets, and for that reason I need to give them the best show possible!

It goes like this:

> *As a storyteller I promise to inspire, entertain, engage, and inform you if you are willing to give me your most valuable and non-renewable asset—your TIME.*

Time is the most valuable gift an audience can give you. You have to respect that. To be clear, this

doesn't mean make your story short, it just means make it powerful and worth it!

Robert Frost says it best with this quote: *"No tears in the writer, no tears in the reader. No surprise for the writer, no surprise for the reader."*[50]

In other words, present it like you want your audience to feel. If you share it flat and boring, then don't expect your audience to feel any different.

I recently facilitated a six-hour story workshop. A group of thirty willingly gave me six hours of their time, their life! That is 180 total hours in the room—time they will never get back! We are talking mortality here! Time that will inevitably take them a little closer to "the end." How can I not give them the best show possible?

That means being provocative, engaging, and energetic. I need to challenge them and get them thinking.

One scientist at P&G calls this being a "constructive deviant."

It's important to challenge comfort. Comfort is not where new ideas spring forth. Comfort is accepting things not because they are the best way, but because they are *the* normal way or sometimes *the* easiest way. *Huge* difference.

Remember MacKenzie's book *Orbiting the Giant*

Hairball? He talks about how inside the "hairball" lives the normal, which is conforming to the accepted models, patterns, processes, or standards. You know what doesn't live in the normal? The original.

You must find the "original," and that is when something is created independent of existing ideas or works. I'll take an audience feeling a bit of discomfort (done the right way) versus sitting there without emotional reactions any day.

So be provocative with your stories!

Sarah Jessica Parker made a statement on *The Howard Stern Show* in 2016 that caught my attention while I was listening. She basically said she always does her best to create a show deserving of the viewers' thirty minutes.

That is a great way to think about your story too. Make your story worth the time people are investing. Be sure to make the "**Storyteller's Promise**" as you create and share your content.

Make it great.

Make it powerful.

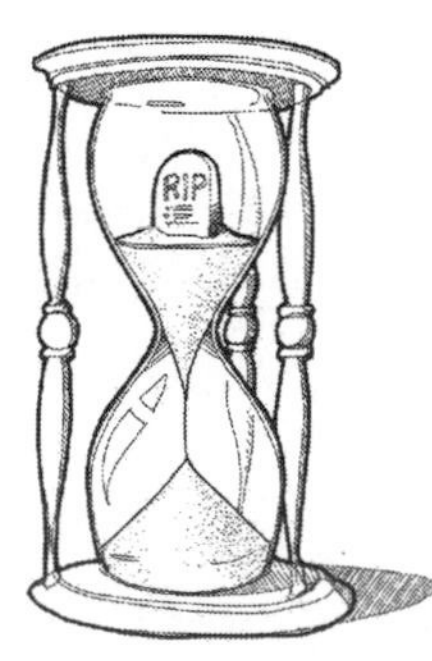

Make it engaging.

Always remember that for anyone to truly engage in your story, they have to give you part of their mortality. Makes you think, doesn't it? Kind of raises the stakes, yes?

Is your content worth part of their life? Make sure you make them feel that it is.

Remember that, and I promise you that your stories and presentations will get better.

Don't sell your story—tell it

One way to fail at the Storyteller's Promise is to use the word *sell*. This is a *very* dangerous word. There's nothing more inauthentic than selling to someone.

Imagine walking up to someone and saying, "Hey, I have something I want to sell you." Think about their reaction. Think about *your* reaction if the roles were reversed. Just mentioning the word "sell" can bring about thoughts of

Lying.

Coercion.

Avoidance.

Manipulation.

Frustration.

We sure love all those "toll-free" calls we get at 8:30 pm from strangers, don't we? Your brain immediately fights back. No one wants to feel *sold* to!

Now, I understand that you're a business and need to sell things to make money. You may even think you need to sell your story. But sales are an outcome—they shouldn't be the means. How, exactly? It's simple.

Just change the first letter of "sell" to a "t."

Don't *sell* your story—*tell* your story.

You are never more authentic than when you are simply telling a story. When you are out with friends at a bar and think to yourself, "Boy, I can't wait to tell them that story!" You don't ever think about "selling" it.

Remember, your kids don't come up to you at night and ask, "Mommy/Daddy, can you pretty please *sell* me a bedtime story?" They want you to *tell* them a great story. They know all too well when it is a "sell" (like when you pick the smaller book or skip sections to speed it up!). A child doesn't want to be "sold" to any more than an adult.

SELL vs TELL

Tell the story you love. Show me the passion you have. It's all a way of thinking and approaching your presentation. If you love your story—if you have passion for it, believe in it—then tell it and let it sell itself.

John Pepper, a previous CEO at P&G, sums it up well:

> Passion and love for a brand and its consumers sustain us. For how can we ever devote our continued highest energy to something if we don't believe in it passionately?[51]
>
> —**John Pepper**

The best stories are told, never sold. If people believe that you really love your story, that you love your content, then giving up that precious *time* we just discussed becomes a lot easier.

They still may not buy, but at least they're engaged—and, in a world of unhelpful noise, that's half of the battle.

Stories de-commodify your brand/product

Ever hear fellow employees use the word "commodity" in association with your brand or products? If you have, you must to put an end to such talk. Because if people in your company think they're making "just a (fill in the blank)," then that's all your brand or products will ever be. It will affect the brand story.

The Always brand doesn't just make feminine pads. They are about protection, providing confidence, and making periods less of a "taboo" to talk about. They are about the realities of femininity, and they are now taking on an even more powerful challenge with the #LikeAGirl story.[52]

Does that sound like a commodity to you? The people who work at Always don't think so! They want to change the world. They want to make a difference.

Similarly, Google doesn't believe it makes just a search engine, Starbucks doesn't believe it makes just coffee, and Nike doesn't believe it makes just shoes.

As the historian for P&G, I know the amount of innovation, time, and passion that go into each and every brand and product we make. They are *not* commodities. They are the blood, sweat, and tears of people set on creating a better life for people all over the globe.

I know that a single product can change someone's life. Let me share an example about my mom.

Ever since she was a little girl, my mom has had trouble with her teeth. Every visit to the dentist was a dreaded trip, because she knew it would end in pain with cavities, root canals, crowns—you name it. And this for a person who takes care of her teeth!

But no matter how often she brushed and flossed, it just didn't make a difference.

Then I happened to meet with a team about the Oral-B toothbrush brand. They showed me a demo of what a power brush could do and how much better they were versus manual ones. I was amazed and decided that I would get my mom the Oral-B 7000 for her upcoming birthday.

She had never used a power brush up until that point, and, let me tell you, she was excited to try it!

A few months later, my phone lit up with my mom's picture during the middle of a story workshop. I was initially concerned, because it wasn't a normal occurrence for her to call me in the middle of the day. So, I asked to step away and answered the phone.

The voice I heard sounded like someone you might think had just won the lottery:

> *Shane, I'm so sorry to bother you in the middle of the day but I had to call. You won't believe it but I just left the dentist and after they did my check up the hygienist said she felt guilty having me come in! I asked, "What do you mean?" She said my teeth were so clean and so plaque free that they felt guilty having me come in! I have never heard that from a dentist office before!*

Does a toothbrush sound like a commodity to you? Not to my mom, and not to me either. She will never part with that Oral-B 7000 (she told me that my stepdad was now using one as well). My brother and my sister-in-law also bought the brush after her story. Good stories spread quickly.

Stop the word "commodity" from showing up in your business. It devalues what you really do. Every product, every ad, every story should be steeped in the Storyteller's Promise. Show how much passion you have for what you do! You are putting your life, your career, and your expertise against your product. If you don't love it, change jobs. Live the story that you want to be remembered for.

We've talked a lot about the meaning of story, the power a story can have, and the importance of telling instead of selling your story.

Moving on, it's time to talk about story mechanics and what's *in* a story.

I call this the Story Recipe.

WORKBOOK

Chapter Seven Questions

Question: What is the unique insight behind your brand?

Question: What story would bring to life the reason why your brand isn't just a commodity?

Chapter Seven Notes

CHAPTER EIGHT

The Story Recipe

What are the ingredients of a great story? Trust me, you know.

Remember how we talked about "practice"? Well, you have had a lot of practice being a story critic. You have seen, read, and heard far more stories than you have probably ever created. You know a good one when you see, read, or hear it.

Here is an exercise I like to start my workshops with. Write down some of the ingredients that all great stories have. See if you can fill in ten:

1.
2.
3.
4.
5.
6.
7.

8.
9.
10.

How many did you think of?

Whatever you put down, this is your list—you created it. So, since this is what you believe all great stories have, I assume that you include all of them in your emails, PowerPoints, summaries, and presentations, right? Well-crafted and memorable? Perfectly executed each time?

No, we both know it's not that easy.

Simply knowing what needs to be present in a great story doesn't really make it any easier to create one. In that sense, it's kind of like cooking: simply knowing the ingredients doesn't guarantee serving a tasty dish.

It's hard to create the next *Casablanca*, the next *Star Wars*, or the next *Silence of the Lambs*. In the same way, it's hard to create the next iPod, the next Starbucks, or the next Facebook.

Like we've explored, it takes a lot of *practice*.

Practice, understanding, and lots of research. It also takes failure and creating bad stories and then learning from them.

You can't just say, "Let's create a great story!" You first have to get everyone up to speed on what a great story is, who it is for, and the kinds of tools that can help you create it. Then you need to practice. Over and over and over again.

Share your ideas. Tear them up. Rebuild them. Writing is also about rewriting.

Rinse, repeat. You get the idea.

Storytelling—a recipe, not a formula

Remember, story is *not* a formula. Formulas are 1+1=2. Analytics, algorithms, clear measurements. Plug things in and out comes a reliably predictable answer. We've gone over it already. Don't look for the formula.

Story is more of a recipe.

Like a recipe, you can plug in all the story ingredients and still end up with some really bad stuff. Give a bad cook the best ingredients and it won't matter. But give a great cook even bad ingredients and they can still create a masterpiece! (Watch the TV show *Chopped* if you don't believe me.) In the end, it is the craft and "know-how" that matter the most. Experience and skill counts. Don't get me wrong, great ingredients can make a huge difference...but you need someone with creativity, insight, and experience to show you how.

I always compare a store-bought apple pie and my grandmother's homemade apple pie. Both use apples, both have crusts, both use sugar, and both are baked. But I would never trade one for the other. My grandma's apple pie has a family story, soul, heritage, memory, secrets, special adds, and hard-won know-how. The other, meanwhile, is automated and made by a predictable, repeated method.

Story is heart, it is craft, it is practice, it is know-how, and it is emotion—just like a good home-baked apple pie recipe handwritten on a card.

If developing a great story were as easy as following a formula, then why are there bad movies and books? If there was a simple formula, every single movie director and writer would have huge hits like James Cameron, John Favreau, Francis Ford Coppola, J. K. Rowling, Aaron Sorkin, or Stephen King.

But these artists have their own recipes for what they do; no two are alike.

If you truly have a distinctive and powerful brand, it's because of your "company recipe"—not a formula. It's your unique way to do that "dish." Recipes are personal, they are customized, they are protected, and passed on by an abiding generational memory.

So are the best brands.

My recipe for a great story

There's an easy side and a hard side to recipes. The easy parts are the ingredients and measurements. The hard part is figuring out what to do with them.

The easy side may proclaim "one cup of sugar," but the hard side may say "add a pinch," or "to your taste." The easy side may say "one TBSP of salt." The hard side may say, "if desired..."

The easy side is objective. The hard side is subjective and, more importantly, *personal.*

I'm going to give you my recipe, the easy side, the ingredients. What I can't give you is the hard side, because craft and style and voice must come from you and you alone. You must take the ingredients and cook them to your audience's taste and add your special know-how.

Here are my five big ingredients:

1. Hero

The hero is the first and the most important ingredient. The hero is the window into the story, the gateway for audience empathy and understanding. Remember, we don't follow plots. We follow characters we can relate to.

If you don't like the hero, the story is over. If you don't think the hero is doing something worthwhile, the story is over. If you don't understand *why* the hero is doing what he or she is doing, the story is over. If you don't care about the hero or their mission, the story is over.

See how important the hero is?

The hero creates meaning in your story.

Meaning is a combination of the values or treasures the hero is seeking, plus the amount of trouble he or she is willing to go through to get it. Nothing ventured, nothing gained.

If the hero is not willing to sacrifice anything to get the treasure, then how powerful can the story be? The key to a successful hero is connection. We must connect with them—we *must* have empathy for the hero.

Empathy is like saying, "I can imagine how that must feel." You can put yourself in the character's shoes and walk in them for a bit. It is seeing with the eyes of another and hearing with the ears of another. It is feeling what they feel.

The main character from *Breaking Bad* is a wonderful example. I deeply empathized with both the internal and external struggles of the hero, Walter White. I could feel the severity of his situation, his moral dilemma, and the fear he faced throughout the first season. To be clear, feeling empathy for him does not make me a meth dealer. Empathy simply puts me in the story to jointly deal with the dilemma that our hero is up against. It forces me to ask, "What would I do in that situation?"

For those of you who didn't see *Breaking Bad*, let me explain the dilemma Walter White was dealing with in the first season.

Walter White was a high school chemistry teacher diagnosed with terminal cancer and given a few months to live. Full stop right there. Can you imagine being given that kind of news? To learn the date of your death? Ask yourself what *you* would do. Would you think about life differently?

See, you're already thinking like the character.

When Walter received the news, he evaluated his life and knew what he needed to focus on—securing his family financially. But it was complicated. His wife had no job, savings were depleted, and his son had cerebral palsy and a lot of medical bills. Oh, and his wife had just told Walter that she was pregnant with their second child.

So, here is the question that *Breaking Bad* posed to its audience: "What would you be willing to do if you only had months left to ensure your family's future financial security?" Unless you have been in that situation, the short answer is: *maybe anything.*[53]

Situations like that put a person in survival mode with a fight or flight response. How often are you in true survival mode? Probably not often. That's why an anti-hero like Walter White can still be someone an audience understands and follows for five whole seasons.

Here is a key principle to remember: You don't have to agree with the hero's solution to the problem (in Walter's case, making the world's purest meth). You just have to understand *why* he did it. *That* is empathy.

And mastering empathy is understanding the human condition.

Once you do that, you can put your hero in any place, time, situation, or emotional state and the audience will be able to understand and feel his struggles with him.

This applies as much to a great movie character as it does to a consumer in a rural village who needs a better and simpler laundry experience to clean her family's clothes.

Who is the hero in your story, how well do you know him or her, and can you make their situation relatable? There are many men who work on products for women and many women who work on products for men. That is empathy—knowing your audience, learning about them, and understanding them. Know who the hero is for your story.

2. Obstacle

The second ingredient is an obstacle.

Obstacles, challenges, and problems are the lifeblood of your story. Without conflict, you have *no* story.

Robert McKee told us all in his class (and in his book), "A protagonist and his (or her)

story can only be as intellectually fascinating and emotionally compelling as the forces of antagonism make them."[54]

It's all about the negative. Whether it's inner or outer conflict, both are massively important to the overall direction and emotional power of your story.

Think about your life for a moment. What stories do you remember the most? The ones where everything went exactly as planned, where you didn't have to deal with unexpected situations? Or do you remember the ones where you were tested, put into dilemmas, forced to take a risk or sacrifice something in an effort to overcome it all? The challenge faced is the key!

Those are the great story moments of our lives.

You may remember a famous book written by a guy named Peter Benchley. It was about this two-foot barracuda that was swimming around the shallows of a town called Amity, occasionally biting people in the ankles.

It was a real nuisance, so the police chief hired a friend of his to catch it. He paid him $25, and his friend went out in the shallows with his rowboat—reel and tackle in hand.

It wasn't easy, though. The man got a little sunburned, spilled his bait bucket, and even got seasick. But he caught the barracuda and brought it back to fry. It was a powerful story. Do you remember that story?

Oh, wait. I got that wrong, didn't I?

Actually, it was about a 25-foot great white shark terrorizing a seaside town called Amity, and the shark's second victim was a child. The main protagonist was a police chief that the town leaders refused to believe because of their greed.

The book was called *Jaws,*[55] and it was also adapted into one of my favorite movies. It was so powerful that, even today, people are afraid to go into the water.

And its power still works, I promise.

Try this. If you are going to the beach soon, watch *Jaws* the night before, and then on that first night go for a nice swim, alone. Once you step into the water, a small voice in your head may remind you that you are not at the top of the food chain. You may even hear a certain haunting soundtrack.

You must have a powerful conflict to truly engage an audience.

In his famous book *The Art of War,* Sun Tzu[56] talks about the power of obstacles, specifically the enemy. He stresses that your "enemy" (call that your competition, the challenge, or maybe the problem you are trying to solve) should be respected as they force you to bring out your best. They help bring about change: change that you may need.

> If you know the enemy and know yourself, you need not fear the result of a hundred battles. If you know yourself but not the enemy, for every victory gained

> you will also suffer a defeat. If you know neither the enemy nor yourself, you will succumb in every battle.[57]
>
> **—Sun Tzu**

Where would Microsoft be without Apple and vice versa? Pampers and Huggies? Coke and Pepsi? The Beatles and the Rolling Stones? P&G has many competitors, and I have always respected and watched all of them, even displaying their products at my desk.

No one has a monopoly on talent or intelligence. Your competitors are all great companies, with great people and great ideas.

Where would you be without *your* competition?

Using dilemma as an obstacle

Be very careful about creating an obstacle based on the choice between a positive and negative. Why? Because the choice between a positive and a negative is probably no choice at all. Who chooses the negative? Example:

Are you good or evil? Do you prefer clean or dirty clothes?

See what I mean?

History's worst monsters all thought they were doing good. No one wakes up and says, "Let's do evil" (unless you're Dr. Evil from the film *Austin Powers*).

To create real story power, you have to go

deeper and find the *dilemma*. That is an obstacle where any choice includes both pros and cons. It could be two necessary evils or dealing with two irreconcilable goods. We can launch that new product a year earlier (which is good) but to do so we will need to invest double the capital (which is not.) The most powerful decisions you have ever made were almost always in a dilemma.

I love coffee, and I want bright white teeth. I know about coffee stains, but I'm not going to give up coffee. Therefore, I am in a dilemma. I have to make a choice. I have to use whitening products (which I pay more for) because I still want to drink my two to three cups of coffee a day.

If Tide is the best detergent out there (which I believe it is), why do inferior options exist (many of which don't come close to the cleaning performance of Tide)? Answer: because people are facing a dilemma.

I could choose Tide, knowing it cleans the best, but to do that I will have to pay more, and maybe I need to put that money somewhere else. In that situation, the consumer is in a dilemma, and there are pros and cons to any decision.

This is why brands must understand the dilemma they are creating for their consumers—and the power that potentially holds. Stories are about choice and change.

The choices that get made and the changes

those choices bring about. When there is a dilemma, it helps amplify that power.

I have seen many products, too many products, that focus on a positive versus a negative choice: full versus empty, expensive versus cheap, safe versus dangerous, clean versus dirty. Again, my problem with those kinds of comparisons is, who would choose the negative state? Nobody—that is not a hard choice and therefore the story will most likely not be strong either. You know your brand is powerful if the consumer is willing to go through some trouble to get it.

The most memorable and powerful decisions we make through life are the ones when the choice isn't easy—we are in a dilemma. We see that in our favorite movies, too.

Let's go back to *Star Wars* for a second. We can find a classic dilemma in Episode V, *The Empire Strikes Back* (my personal favorite). As Luke was battling Darth Vader, he knew that if he could beat him, it would be a huge step to bringing peace back to the galaxy. But, out of nowhere, Darth Vader tells Luke a single, previously unknown fact: "I am your Father." *What?* Now that created quite the dilemma!

It still is one of cinema's most jaw-dropping moments. It wasn't just deciding if good should fight evil—that is easy. Now each choice had the potential for a positive and a negative outcome. He could kill Darth Vader and rid the universe of evil, but to do that he would also need to kill his father! Or he could finally be with his father (whom he had never met and longed to know more about), but to do so he would have to join the Dark Side and go against his beliefs.[58] What to do, what to do?

Those are the kind of choices that make stories memorable. That scene is permanently burned into my memory and is part of the cultural lexicon. Everyone knows that scene and that line even if they don't follow *Star Wars*.

That is what understanding dilemma can do. Just always remember, if your product or brand solves a weak problem, it most likely will be a weak story.

3. Treasure

The third ingredient is a treasure. Every hero needs a proper motivation, a treasure worthy of the journey and of their sacrifice. Do you know what your hero really wants? Here is a basic story principle: people really won't do anything if there isn't a proper reward at the end. That doesn't mean they are lazy, it means they are making a choice. We can't go after everything.

In economics, this is called cost-benefit analysis: assessing whether the benefit of a decision or action outweighs its costs, which may be tangible or intangible. It works the same in stories. Therefore, the goal, the outcome, the objective, or the treasure becomes important in influencing the hero to spend that precious energy.

Have you ever seen the picture of a person on the back of a donkey, holding a fishing pole with a carrot dangling from it? Well, we are the donkey, always looking for life's carrots. For us to spend our time and energy, there must be something for us to gain, something emotional, spiritual, physical, mental, or financial—there *must* be a reward.

What prevents you from going on every journey put in front of you? It's simple: the treasure just doesn't feel worth it. The right treasure can make a hero willing to endure tremendous risk, danger, or even failure. In other words, the best treasure makes the hero willing to go through any obstacle to get it. You therefore must know what would properly motivate your hero. What do they *really* want? Again, *research*!

Now, there are often two different types of treasures: treasures that represent a change for the moment and those that bring a change in life. The moral to the story or the bigger lesson is clearly more of a change in life.

Tiffany is a great brand with a powerful story. It is a brand that is part of many of life's big moments.

Weddings, anniversaries, holidays, and other special occasions. It is one of my wife's favorites. Like any great treasure, there are obstacles in the path of getting it—waiting for the right occasion, going to the store, choosing the right piece of jewelry, and deciding how much to spend.

Each obstacle is worth every bit of struggle when you see the person light up at the sight of the little blue box. That blue color has tremendous meaning to many because of that powerful story.

So, the actual piece of jewelry is a change in moment, but the role it plays in what it represents is the change in life.

Speaking of rings, one of my favorite characters named Frodo had to deal with one as well. Frodo endured many horrific physical and emotional obstacles, not to get a ring but to destroy it in Mount Doom.

Why did he go through so much turmoil and anguish? So much sacrifice? Because the ring's destruction would bring peace to Middle-earth. It would also save his friends and, most importantly, his homeland, the Shire.

The destruction of the ring would be the change in moment, but the overall peace and safety that would come from that would be the change in life.[59]

It is essential that you know your hero and what reward would truly move them.

4. Climax

The fourth ingredient is a climax. You need a powerful catharsis and resolution to your story that satisfies the audience. What are you building up to?

There is a simple visual you can use to lay out the emotional path of your story. A graph with one axis called Emotion and the other Time.

The trick in storytelling is to keep raising the emotional stakes for both the hero and your audience. The further you go in the story, the more emotion you need to build. Doing that helps keep the audience's attention.

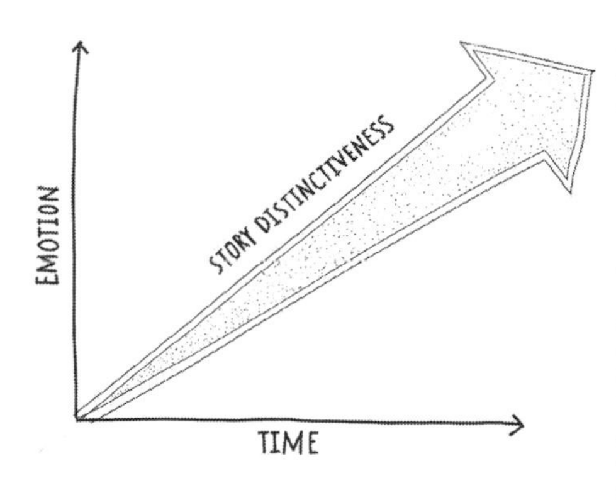

If slide ten of your PowerPoint is the most impactful and emotional moment of your forty-slide deck, you're in big trouble. Why would your audience want to see anything after slide ten if that is the climactic moment? This is why big battles in movies are usually at the end. This is why it took seven books before Harry really fought Voldemort and three movies before Frodo and Sam destroyed the ring.

Now in order to achieve this, you have to plan out and manage the emotion in your story. It's like the beat and tempo in a song, and you have to keep building it up and save the best for last.

C. C. Deville's great solo in "Nothin' but a Good Time" happens in the last third of the song (as do most guitar solos). The song starts with a great hook riff, then the lyrics set up what the song is about. It finishes off with a bridge and then a killer guitar solo, slowly letting the curtain drop with repeating the chorus and a fade out of: *"Don't need nothin' but a good time and it don't get better than this."*[60]

Using the three-act structure to plan your story climax

As the story moves on, you need to keep your audience's interest, and to do that, you need to create more impact. That does not mean you should have more explosions and more special effects—those do not equal emotion. The story needs depth and dilemma, not just spectacle. Aristotle said that you need a good beginning, middle, and end.

That is often called the three-act structure. You can have more than three acts, but it is a great model to understand and leverage.

Think of the beginning as "set-up." What is the minimum the audience needs to know and understand to engage with the story? How are you setting up what is out of balance in the hero's life?

The middle is all about challenges and obstacles. The middle is the meat of the story. What are the key tests, obstacles, and conflicts for your hero? What allies and mentors will help them? What challenges will they face, and how will they move the story forward?

The ending is all about resolution. It is where the climactic moment will occur. It is all about delivering the story's meaning and moral to both the hero and the audience. The climax's epiphany can be handled overtly or covertly. You can blurt it out or you can ask the audience to read between the lines.

For example, sometimes in life it can take a long time before you realize what the lesson really was for something. It's like when you look back on an old project, or maybe an old boss, and finally understand what you learned from them and how that moment changed you.

I grew up on a farm and always helped my grandfather around the property—digging out and replacing drainage tile, picking up rocks in the field to prepare for planting, mowing, pond maintenance, fence repair—there were always projects to be done.

I also started working outside of the farm when I was fourteen, across a very wide variety of jobs and types of work ranging from a stone company to a power company meter reader.

My parents used to tell me how important it was to be a hard worker and to do every job, whether you liked it or not, to the best of your ability. They told me to take pride in "the job" and to always show that you were someone who would deliver no matter the situation.

As a teenager that wasn't always what I wanted to hear, but I did it. The treasure I really wanted and understood at that moment was simply getting paid (that was the "change in moment"). However, there was a bigger lesson to be learned. My story was just getting started. I would realize that lesson when I started to think about my career.

When I was just a sophomore in design school, I applied for an internship with P&G Design Department. I obviously did not have a lot of design experience yet but was excited to learn. Many of the questions they asked me during the interview included things like, "Tell me about a time that you showed leadership in a job," "Explain how you have dealt with a difficult work situation in the past," or "Tell me about a time that you failed at something and what you learned from it."

All those different jobs I'd had since I was young prepared me for those questions, especially since I did all of them to the best of my ability. I had stories from each of them and, most importantly, lots of people who would back me up (references). I got that P&G internship and was offered a full-time position two years later.

Now when I look back, the bigger lesson and moral to the story (the "change in life") was that my parents knew that someone who is dependable and hardworking, someone who takes pride in their job, is someone companies look for. They were helping me develop a strong work ethic.

Today I am teaching my kids that same lesson, sharing my examples and hoping they stick. It is not the job you have as a kid that is important. It's how you behave when you are there and the work ethic you build that really makes the difference. I know that if they learn this lesson, they will find a great job someday too.

See how that short story about being a hard worker led up to the climax of me being at P&G and then sharing what I learned with my kids? It had a brief setup, a conflict, and a resolution. Importantly, the end was the most powerful part.

Doug Heyes, a well-known TV writer, has a great quote I remind myself of as I work on developing brand story climaxes and emotional build up:

> What's happening now must be inherently more interesting than what just happened.[61]
>
> **—Doug Hayes**

Again, that doesn't mean make something "loud" or "noisy" for the sake of trying to be distinctive, but instead to escalate the emotion properly and to make each scene stronger than what preceded it (or at minimum, each scene must help eventually build to a stronger scene). Manage your story's emotional rhythm. The stakes have to increase. The emotion has to increase, or interest will eventually be lost.

5. Transformation

The last ingredient is one of my favorites. It is transformation. In simple words, you need a powerful "before" and "after" for the hero. How does your hero transform from the beginning to the end? What does he or she learn? If your hero is exactly the same at the end as in the beginning, then your story went nowhere!

Luke started out as a naive, headstrong moisture farmer who felt trapped on Tatooine, but by the end of the story he was the savior of the rebellion, in control of his own destiny, and on the path to becoming a Jedi.[62]

Now that is change and transformation!

When it comes to your brand or a product, ask yourself this: How do my consumers feel before they use our product, and how do I want them to feel after? You have to plan for that.

Now, don't answer that with the word "good." "They feel good" is *not* a good answer. Moving from *bad* to *good* is a weak journey. It is a choice between a negative and a positive. It lacks power.

Go deeper than that.

Having a strong holistic story experience for your brand is not just about having consistency in the message, it is also about making your consumers a part of the journey. It's about helping them move from a weaker "before" to a stronger "after." That doesn't mean the before was "bad" though. Consumers can always find products that deliver the benefits they seek. But if you create a powerful transformation, it will ensure that the experiences you create around your product truly bring about change and memorability.

I bet most of you reading this book have a device called a "smartphone." You may even have the one I am loyal to: the iPhone. I am old enough to remember what my life was like before I had an iPhone (or even a cell phone, for that matter). Before I had either, I was able to find my friends, was comfortable using payphones, and found people's addresses using paper maps stored in my glove compartment. It worked. It wasn't "bad." It was just the way it was done. At the time, it also felt convenient.

But then I got an iPhone, and everything changed. Is today a stronger emotion than before? Yes. But, did that come easy? No. I had to learn a lot, change my behaviors, and spend a lot of money.

To understand the transformation that has happened in society because of the iPhone, try this exercise: take your smartphone and put it away for two months. Two months!? Try two days! Heck, for some of you, try two hours!

Do you see the emotional and habitual difference a product can make? The transformation you have gone through over the last several years because of the iPhone is profound. You probably can't imagine going back to a life without it. That is the key in a strong transformation.

That is power, and that means it has a great story.

If you take the product away and the hero feels an emotional change or shift (pain, loss, anxiety, fear, etc.), then you have created something powerful. You have created something that they now have an attachment to. That they see it as a needed tool for the journey they are on.

In other words, if I took away your iPhone and hid it for two months, would you feel "loss" or "anxiety" or "discomfort" or "anger" or "frustration" or even "fear"? If yes to any, then it is a great transformation story. The hero doesn't want to go back to the way he or she was before they had it.

On the other hand, if I take a product or brand away from you and you feel the same with or without it, then what power does the story have?

Not much, the story is weak.

The transformation doesn't have to be complicated, either. What was the transformation in *The Wizard of Oz*? You know it—just think of the famous last line: "There's no place like home." The transformation in that film is a simple one. It is about a pissed off teenager who needs to learn an important lesson. A lesson every teen has to learn at some point.

Dorothy starts off upset because her family won't protect her little dog from that mean lady. She felt unsupported by her family (we have all felt that at some point). So, like all teenagers when they get upset, Dorothy thinks to herself, "I don't need them—I will run away." But shortly after she leaves, she realizes it's not easy and that home is much better. She decides to go back. But then a twister hits and she is taken away.

As soon as she lands in Oz, her first big question upon meeting Glinda is, "How do I get home?" Not to explore Oz, not to stay for a few weeks and see the sights, not to meet all the people, not to get a map and find the best hotels. She wants to go *home*.

She then goes through obstacle after obstacle and eventually wakes up in Kansas with her family around her and utters that famous, iconic last line.[63]

The transformation that Dorothy makes is simply to go from not appreciating home and how great it is to the realization that there is no place like it.

So, how do your consumers feel before using your brand, and then after? Is the transformation powerful? Does it leave a lasting mark on them? Can they imagine life without you or would they want to go back to the way things were before? These are the questions that can help you see if your story has power.

Once you have changed consumers with your product, one of the hardest things to do is to then create a great sequel (your next product) that continues to transform their lives in unexpected ways. A story that continues the original's strong transformation but also brings something new to the table.

This challenge is the same for a long-term innovation pipeline or the next advertising campaign, and it is a challenge in the film world as well. As you start to plan your larger brand story, you can learn a lot by studying movie sequels and how the best ones keep raising the bar and what the bad ones usually suffer from. We will talk more about that later.

So, there are the five key story ingredients. Practice them, play with them, and experiment. Remember, it is like cooking. All these are just ingredients; both good and bad movies usually have them all. The difference is in the craft and how it's all put together. The unique insight in the story, the understanding, and any special "flavor" added. It is also critical that *your* personality is in the story. That is what I call the secret spice.

Your secret spice

The best recipes always have a secret spice. It is the special cinnamon that my grandma would add to her apple pie, even though it wasn't written down in the recipe.

Remember Valerie Lapointe's (Pixar) quote about your true super power (from Chapter One)? It is your unique perspective. It is your life story and how you see things. Don't lose that. Make sure your story sounds like you and reflects your personality. How will you bring your personal style to the story? What are your signature story elements? You should know the story you want to tell better than anyone. What is your brand's secret spice? What makes it unique?

Again, just because you have all the ingredients we talked about doesn't mean the dish will taste any good. That simply takes practice and a study of the craft. It takes testing and feedback. You will fail, and some of your stories will be bad. That is all part of learning.

The next section is about how to put all the elements together. That is called a story structure: the bones underneath your narrative.

WORKBOOK

Chapter Eight Questions

Question: Who is your hero, and what is out of balance in their life? What are the obstacles they must face? What treasure is motivating them to go on the journey? What is the climactic moment of your story? What is the hero's before and after (transformation) and what did they truly learn?

____

____

____

____

____

____

____

____

Question: What is your "secret spice"? How do you bring your unique perspective into your stories?

Chapter Eight Notes

CHAPTER NINE

The Single Story Structure

There is an old saying in Hollywood—stories are about chasing the hero up a tree, throwing rocks at them, and seeing how they will get down. That is pretty much it, right? There is a lot of detail missing in there of course, a lot of the "whys" and "hows," but overall that is the general flow of almost every movie I can think of (metaphorically speaking). If you want to understand the idea of story structure, you need to check out the work of Joseph Campbell. His book is what made me realize that the principles of screenwriting could be applied to any business or brand problem.

The most influential part of his book (*The Hero with a Thousand Faces*) was his explanation of an idea called the "mono-myth," a single story structure. Now, there are many different examples of story structures out there by many different artists, writers, and filmmakers, and I am not here to tell you that Campbell's is right and the others are wrong. Check them all out! But it was his that really helped me see the true connections between stories and the importance of understanding the basic concept of story structures.

Joseph Campbell was a comparative mythologist. He studied all the cultural mythologies from around the world: The stories people created to explain the ideas and rituals they had established across generations, the rules and reasoning they used, and how they explained the key questions about life itself. Most of these cultures were separated by vast oceans, searing deserts, and mountain-covered landscapes, and yet they all had something in common.

As he examined these stories, he noticed a skeleton framework that all the stories seemed to have followed. Across time, religions, regions, and cultures, people were telling very similar stories—just changing the executions and expressions to make them regionally and culturally relevant. In other words, human beings like to tell stories in a certain way, and he called it the *Hero's Journey*.

It basically went like this:

> A Hero ventures forth from the world of the common day into a region of supernatural wonder. Fabulous forces are encountered and a decisive victory is won. The hero returns from this adventure to bestow boons

> on his fellow man.[64]
>
> **—Joseph Campbell**

Very poetic, very simple, and incredibly clear. Try to think of a story you love that does not fit into that sentence in some way. Now, be careful with this, as it is not a "plug and play" construct or template. It is essentially a skeleton to help hold the story up. Story structures are like bones. We all have the same ones, but we all look different, too. The basic structure of a story is infinitely flexible in expression.

So, this structure can help you lay out your story and it can provide support, but you still have to make sure it is a good one and decide the best way to bring it to life.

While Campbell's Hero's Journey model had seventeen stages, another brilliant story theorist named Christopher Vogler (author of *The Writer's Journey*, which is also one of my favorites) simplified it to twelve.

Years ago, I took both of their seminal works and reduced their models to seven stages for my story workshops. I will share that in a later chapter. For now, let me give my one-sentence version. Yep, just one sentence.

> **Every Hero must go through an Obstacle to get to a Treasure.**

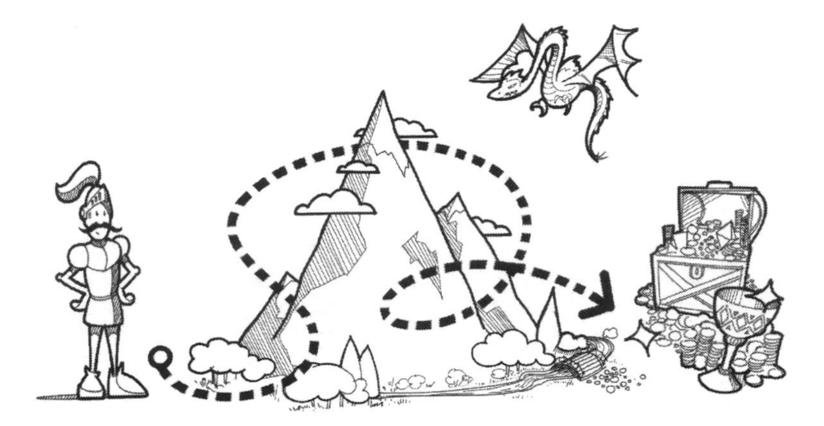

This is every story I have ever told or that has ever been told to me. This sentence is *The Dark Knight* and *Ratatouille*. It is you explaining why you are late to work, or why you need to get rid of Voldemort, how your company will meet next quarter's earnings, or why Frodo must destroy the ring of power. It is you deciding on a career path, what job to take, or how to deploy a new organizational structure. It is the spinal column of a story.

It reminds me that all the songs have been sung—it's just a matter of how you will sing them differently today. There are only twelve notes of music, after all. Beethoven and Justin Bieber use the same twelve, but isn't it amazing how they can be combined in totally different ways?

Pocahontas, *Dances with Wolves*, *FernGully*, *The Last Samurai*, and *Avatar* are the same basic story, but they are each brought to life differently and uniquely.

Hero, obstacle, treasure

This basic drawing was first shared and sketched out for me by a friend and mentor of mine, David Kuehler (thanks again, David!). David was a colleague at P&G many years ago and was the leader of our Clay Street facility when it was first built (a place dedicated to changing how teams work and leveraging new methods of problem solving; just Google "P&G Clay Street" to read more).

I was part of one of the early Clay Street Project teams, and one day David sketched this visual using a stick figure, triangle, and chalice on a chart pad. From that moment, I was hooked. I immediately started seeing tons of places I could use this and how it connected with all the story research I was doing at the time.

This has become one of my most indispensable tools to help teams begin the story process. I always start projects by filling in the blanks of this visual—who is the hero, what are the obstacles (the physical and emotional, the obvious and the unknown), and what are the treasures the hero seeks (internal and external, the small and the big).

It is a tool to help explore potential story lines and to take a quick look at the differences between them. Interestingly, it also showed me that there is no such thing as a single story. What matters is *whose eyes* you plan on telling the story through.

Let me discuss a movie example using the sketch.

With the overall objective of destroying the ring of power and bringing peace to Middle-earth, let's say I put Frodo in the hero spot and I then filled in the many obstacles he faced and the treasures he discovered. No problem.

Then, right under Frodo's name I add a new hero, Gandalf. Then I write down Gandalf's obstacles and treasures. Then Sam, Aragorn, and so on and so forth.

Did they all want the same thing in the end, the same basic thing that Frodo also wanted? Sure they did, peace in Middle-earth. But, did they all have the exact same obstacles and treasures? They did not. So, again, there is no such thing as one story. It's just deciding whose eyes you are going to tell it through and, most importantly, whose eyes will make it the most powerful.

Could J. K. Rowling have told the *Harry Potter* stories from Hermione, Dumbledore, or Ron's perspectives? Sure, but none of them were the "the boy who survived" or the "chosen one." You could also tell the *Harry Potter* story from Snape's perspective. But J. K. Rowling decided to tell it from Harry's perspective, which makes the most sense and harnesses the most power.

Hero, obstacle, treasure in brand stories

For a business application example, let's say your company is moving to a new organizational structure and you plan on sharing the reason at an upcoming deployment meeting. As you are creating the presentation, sketch out the Hero-Obstacle-Treasure visual and fill in the blanks.

Start by listing the different heroes in your company, maybe groups like "R&D," "Finance," and "Marketing." Perhaps you want to think about specific types of employees like "new hires" or "old guard." Maybe you need to also plan how you will explain the change to "external shareholders." You get the idea. Each of these heroes will have different obstacles and treasures to be aware of for the same organizational change. Presenting the detailed reasons for change will be different for each, particularly on how it will affect them and their work.

What about for a brand or product? In the visual above, which one of those pictures is your brand or product? Is it the hero? Is it the treasure? For sure you hope it is not the obstacle!

Well, let me tell you two things that you should never deliberately make your brand—the hero *or* the treasure, and here is why. It can't be the treasure because the consumer is usually looking for something higher level that your brand may help deliver (e.g., clean clothes, confidence, dandruff-free hair, portable music, easy-to-use computer, accessibility, empowerment, etc.), but there are many ways to get that without your specific brand. The treasure is a much higher meaning or need versus any single product.

The brand is also not the hero! If the brand is the hero, then where is your consumer in the story? If you make the brand or product the hero, you have just removed your consumer from the journey. By definition (Merriam-Webster online), "a hero is a *person* who is admired for great or brave acts or fine qualities."[65] So, that means my phone, my running shoes, or my detergent can't be the hero!

Heroes have to be people, not things. So, the hero is always the user, the customer, or the consumer. Calling your brand "the protagonist" makes no sense. The consumer is the one on the journey of life, not the product.

A brand or product is an inanimate object and there is not a product made that can do anything without a consumer's hands to buy it, learn it, and use it. Products and brands serve and help the people who use them. At P&G there is a saying that is repeated over and over: "The consumer is boss."

In great stories, we need a hero with a powerful struggle whom we can identify with and who will be the source of empathy we can design a product toward. The product simply becomes a tool for the hero.

Internally, you can't think of the brand as the hero either, because in the end, the consumer won't care what the brand's struggles are and no consumer has empathy for a brand's innovation problems—they care about the final solution and how it will *help them*.

It is their struggle that must be your inspiration. Help them by giving them the tools for their journey.

That's the real role of your company, brand, or product. In the world of story, that is a character called the Mentor.

Every hero needs a mentor

Every story has some sort of mentor that, unlike a hero, doesn't have to be a person. A lot of the time, mentors appear right before or right after the trouble really starts for the hero.

Heroes often get their inspiration, tools, and information about the challenge from the mentor in the story. A mentor is "a trusted counselor or guide" (Merriam-Webster online).[66] Mentors can be a magazine article, a book, a quote, a TED Talk, an observation, a friend, your conscience, a speech, or a brand. It can be a lot of things.

All mentors in stories play two key roles: 1) to guide and inspire the hero, and 2) to provide the hero with some sort of "item" to help them past the obstacles they may face. Isn't that what companies

and brands do?

Companies, brands, and products are *mentors*, providing guidance and inspiration to their consumers and giving them items to help them get past the many obstacles of life—from the small to the big.

Your customers and consumers are the real heroes—and your role is to help them.

In Tide ads, a child may get his baseball uniform dirty before picture day and then give it to Mom to fix. When it comes out spotless, the kid doesn't run past Mom and go to the washroom and hug the bottle—he hugs Mom! Tide is a tool for her. She is the real hero who deals with the dirty uniform.

Similarly, the Mr. Clean character doesn't clean the crayon marks off the wall for the consumer. He hands the Magic Eraser to them, so *they* can. He is there to help but he knows he can't do the work. The consumer is the hero of the story.

I am a runner. Not professionally or anything, just for exercise. But I run three times a week and really enjoy it. Running is part of who I am. I am *very* loyal to my running shoes (as most runners are). Once you get a pair that feels right, it becomes part of your ritual, part of your running identity.

Let's be clear though, the shoes don't wake me up to go and run. They don't pat me on the back as I am running. They don't remind me that exercise is healthy—none of that. They are a tool, a lightsaber of sorts, to help me past the obstacles of knee pain, uncomfortable runs, and improper gear.

The shoe is not the hero. I, the consumer, am the one who has to have the motivation, dedication, commitment, and willingness to get up and run whether it is cold or hot outside. The shoe doesn't make any of those decisions.

I am also a backpacker, and I *am very loyal* to Mountain Hardwear tents and backpacks! I have a story about that, which I will share in a later chapter. But, again, let's be clear, the tent is not the hero. I am the one who carries it on my back for twenty-four miles, sets it up, takes care of it, stores it, and practices how to pack it up efficiently. I don't go backpacking to be in a tent. The tent is one of my many tools to enjoy the real meaning of my journey, which is the peace, beauty, and serenity of nature.

Mountain Hardwear is a great brand and never tries to tell me that the tent is the hero. Instead they show people enjoying the outdoors, enjoying the journey, and the tent is just a great tool to help them get there.

Who wouldn't want to be Obi-Wan Kenobi or Glinda the Good Witch anyway? This means that what you really make for your consumers are lightsabers and ruby slippers!

Be a mentor and help your hero.

The sole purpose of a mentor should be to help the hero move forward. That should also be your goal as someone who makes any product or service. P&G is always striving to better understand and help their consumers with products that will do the job needed and deliver superior results. This then allows consumers to focus on what is most important: their family, their friends, and their life.

Just like the P&G Olympic "Thank You Mom" ad shows: Moms do all the work in taking their kids to practice, washing their clothes, preparing their meals, and providing the love, support, and dedication their children need; P&G products just try to simplify her list where they can.

So, there you go, my story structure and mentor model can be a helpful planning tool, but it also will not write the story for you. It is not a silver bullet. It is there to help try different story arcs and to iterate against. It is a prototyping tool.

Like any tool, the Hero's Journey is not for everyone. You need to use what works for you. Like I said earlier, there are a lot of other story structure theories out there. Use what you want. To be fair though, I have yet to watch a movie that didn't feature Campbell and Vogler's steps in some way. They aren't always in linear order, and they are not always used the exact same way, but that is the point of a good tool—it's also flexible. The deeper values that the stages represent are always present (as far as I can tell), and that is what you have to look for.

Campbell never promised you could plug items into his model and it would spit out a timeless classic. He simply recognized what all stories are really about—*life*. That is what the Hero's Journey is about. What other stories do people ever tell? Every story is about life.

Practice this simple story structure and you will see benefits quickly (just don't try and turn it into a magic template).

Practice, practice, practice. But, what about when you need to start planning the next story? How will you ensure that it tops your first? What will you do for your next product launch?

Using story as a planning strategy starts with understanding and learning from the movie version of "your next product"—that is called a sequel.

WORKBOOK

Chapter Nine Questions

Question: Choose a project from work and write down the different heroes that your story needs to understand. Which one makes the most sense to focus the larger story on? Why?

____

____

____

____

____

____

____

____

Question: Who is the mentor in your story, and how do they guide and inspire? What do they provide the hero to help with the obstacle(s) ahead?

Chapter Nine Notes

CHAPTER TEN

Movie and Brand Sequels

Many stories are a single act: one movie, play, or book and then they are done.

But many others are part of a larger story and are extended, grown, and evolved. These are called sequels. When I think of a sequel in brand or product terms, it is whatever your next initiative is.

A company or brand is made up of *many* sequels. In fact, I think brands should stop using the words "initiative" or "project" and start calling them "sequels." That is what they are, and it helps change your approach.

Now, there are essentially two kinds of sequels—the planned and the forced.

A planned sequel is exactly how it sounds: from the beginning, there was a larger story at play. Then there are the forced sequels. Those usually happen because the first film or book was such a success that the studio or publisher immediately asked if another one was possible. Sometimes those turn out really good. But many of them can end up looking contrived or low-quality. Coincidentally, both kinds can make money and be profitable. But, as I said before, making money doesn't mean it is a good story.

And here's the thing: we don't need more stories, we need more *great* stories!

Over the last twenty-plus years, sequels have been *very* popular. In fact, after looking at the data on the site "The Numbers: Where Data and the Movie Business Meet," a majority of the top ten highest-grossing films since 1995 have been "sequel-like" films. (Note: I am using the word *sequel* broadly to cover anything that was based on previous material, such as book adaptations, reboots,

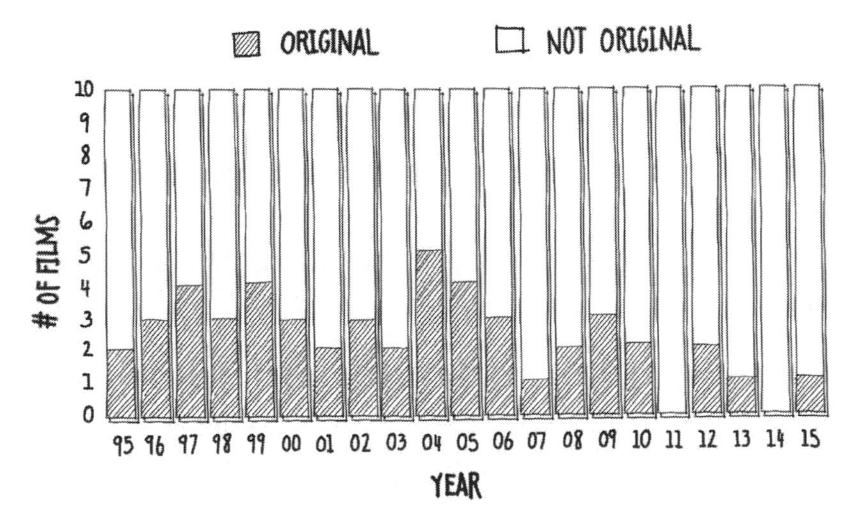

traditional sequels, or extensions.) Whatever you think of sequels, they are very popular![67]

Why do you need a sequel?

There are many advantages to sequels. The first is familiarity: you probably know your audience well. Also, your story and characters are well established. So, you don't need to spend as much time on setup and teaching people about them (try and find someone who doesn't know who Darth Vader is or a brand like Pampers or Starbucks). Lastly, you probably have a preexisting fan base that can help create buzz for your next stories.

It works the same with brands, too. Look at brands like Apple or Tide. Do all of the above apply when they launch their next product? Absolutely. Consumers know Tide is a leader. They know it is high quality and that it has a strong heritage. Tide doesn't have to remind every consumer of its longstanding reputation and dependability. Everyone already knows Tide has been around for a long time, and that can be a great advantage to have over a new-to-the-world brand.

However, there are also disadvantages to doing a sequel. The biggest one is that it is a lot tougher to surprise the audience when you do a part two, three, five, etc. For example, Yankee Candle or Febreze launching a new scent will probably not be a shock to their fan base. With sequels, your fans know your story, know your characters, and know your brand's "rules," and they will expect you to usually adhere to them. For example, Jason Bourne can't suddenly go to outer space, no matter how distinctive and exciting the studio may think that would be. That is just not part of his story line.

Your fan base holds high expectations when you do a sequel (assuming the first one was good). If they loved your first movie and have an attachment to the characters and story line, they probably can't wait to see where it goes next—so, you'd better deliver.

Lastly, let's be honest, it is pretty tough to beat the original. That goes for books, music, movies, or anything for that matter. Just ask Coca-Cola what happens when you change the original.[68]

But, it can be done!

Planning your sequel

When it comes to sequels, the first thing you need to do is plan them early. Get your team together as early as possible and make sure they are ready to roll up their sleeves. Sequel planning is, and should be, very hard work. In fact, if your long-term launch plan and sequel strategy is easy, then I'm not sure you did it right or have thought through all the details.

How often are sequels better than the original? Not often! Outdoing what you have already done is not easy (and it shouldn't be). But a great sequel, when done well, can extend, advance, and grow what the original did in incredible ways.

It's the same with products and brand extensions.

So, the question with a sequel is what kind do you want in your legacy—*The Godfather II* or *Paul Blart Mall Cop II*?

I have an entire workshop I do with teams to help them create what I call a "brand sequel map." Here are a few principles to consider before you start your next brand sequel:

1. Do you even need a sequel?

This is the most important question. The last thing people want is more products. What they need are more products that make a difference and make life better. Anybody can just launch something. The same goes for sequels.

Great sequels *challenge* the story, they take it to new places. They don't just keep *matching* what's been done before. Whereas *Friday the 13th* really kept matching the same story, *Toy Story* kept challenging and evolving the story while also staying true to itself.

So, ask yourself, "Is my new product challenging and evolving the story or just repeating what has already been done?" Are you raising the emotional bar? Should you extend this brand or product? Start with that hard question. Maybe you need to extend the brand into a totally different place or even create a new brand.

2. Create something new while also understanding your brand's hard and soft points.

Assuming the story should be extended, maintaining the most powerful parts of the original will be important. That is your *mythos* (i.e., your brand beliefs, your core mythology). Respect the previous story and build from there. You have to know your character, or the brand character, inside and out so that there is *never* a question of what must be kept and what can change.

Character and story equities are *not* very elastic and shouldn't be. Stretch them too far and they'll break, making the sequel look "forced" or "cheap."

Another way to look at this is knowing your brand's hard and soft points. What is more or less fixed and what is more flexible?

For example, there are certain things that are a given part of the *Indiana Jones* mythos. Hard points would be his dress code (leather jacket and fedora), what he carries (bullwhip), his unrelenting courage, curiosity, and his passion for adventure. Even the time period is a hard point. He could never carry a taser, be a coward, or be put in suspended animation to awaken in the 2000s. A soft point may be the kind of historic artifact he is after, the city the adventure takes place in, or the clever ways he gets out of trouble. Those aspects of the story can be changed without tainting the *Indiana Jones* mythos. Tide is orange with an iconic bull's-eye, Nike uses a swoosh, and Tiffany is in a blue box with a white ribbon. Those are hard points.

3. Ensure the new villain (problem) is stronger and more interesting than the previous one.

I've noticed one key insight about sequels. The power of the second, third, and fourth films seems to be directly related to the power of the "villain" that the hero is up against. Much like the obstacle being the lifeblood of your story, the villain is the lifeblood of your sequel. A weak problem for the hero will usually equal a weak story.

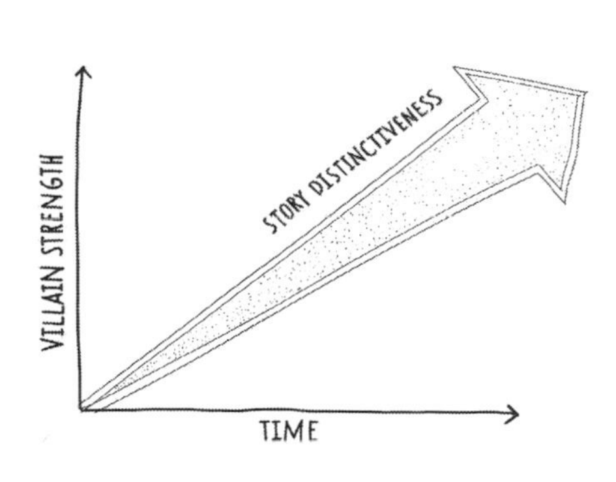

A "villain" in brand terms is the same as the job to be done, the problem that needs solving, the consumer tension, or the key obstacle they must face. If the problem your brand just solved was a big one and the next problem is small, then that is exactly how it will look: *small*—which can make it feel less inspiring to your hero and audience. It can create a *"so what?"* effect.

Let's talk some of the big problems that Apple sequels faced:

- When the Macintosh launched, it showed us how computers could be easy to use and that we didn't have to learn MS-DOS.

- When the iMac launched, it showed us that technology could be beautiful and well-designed (versus ugly, grey plastic boxes with lots of wires).

- When the iPod launched, it revolutionized music and put 1,000 songs in our pocket (versus the ten or so that disc players gave us).

- When the iPhone launched, it set the bar for all smartphones through an incredible interface, design, an app store, and superior technology.

These not only changed the consumer but also the entire category of each product. Each tackled a very powerful villain and kept increasing the brand emotion.

I can't stress this point enough! The obstacle/villain is the lifeblood and will decide how powerful your sequel will be. Let's discuss a few well-known movie sequels and a brand example to show you what I mean.

The first *Die Hard* had Hans Gruber as the villain (what a villain—clever, witty, dangerous and deceptive). *Die Hard 2*, the one in the airport, featured Colonel William Stewart as the villain, but he didn't escalate the story with the same intensity. Then came the third *Die Hard* (*Die Hard with a Vengeance*) with the Simon character. To try to elevate him, they made him Hans's brother and portrayed him as a villain seeking revenge, but he still wasn't Hans (and his plan wasn't really any different; it was all about misleading the police through trickery again).

Similarly, *Jaws* was incredible. But, *Jaws 2*? It was good. I liked *Jaws 2*, but it wasn't like seeing *Jaws* for the first time, mostly because I knew from the get-go what was going to happen. And don't get me started on *Jaws 3* and *Jaws 4*.

Then we have the Christopher Nolan Batman movies—in my opinion, the best of the best when it comes to the many Batman films. The first, with Ra's al Ghul, was great; the second, with the Joker, was absolutely incredible; the third one, with Bane, was fantastic! It is an example of a trilogy that really delivered and kept building, challenging each previous film.

The James Bond films, meanwhile, appeared to be in trouble in the early 2000s. Audiences and critics were seeing too much of the same everything—same look and feel, lots of explosions and exotic locales, impossible traps, and lots of women. James Bond himself had become an indestructible, superhero-like figure. It had become a formula. Worst of all, the villains were becoming flat, often with the same "world domination" objective.

But then it got a bold, fresh reboot with *Casino Royale,* one of the best Bond films.

My favorite, though, is *Skyfall*, with the incredible villain Raoul Silva (played by Javier Bardem). The conflict he created and brought to the film, along with his personal relationship with both Bond and M, was incredible and created the reason for the story.

I am reminded of what McKee says about the Obstacle: "The protagonist can only be as powerful as the forces of antagonism allow him or her to be!"[69]

Using the same model, look at your brand and the "villain" that each of your key products tackled. Are your products moving up the emotional axis? Are the challenges getting more powerful as you go? Take Swiffer as a great example. It first launched in 1998 and changed the world of cleaning forever using its unique dry sheets armed with static. The villains were brooms pushing the dirt around. Swiffer was a fast way to get the dirt and dust up off the floor.

WetJet then launched and changed mopping forever as a wonderful all-in-one solution.

Then Dusters launched and gave people a better dusting experience through a reduction of steps (no more spray and rags) and new ergonomics. It also helped dust the hardest-to-reach places. Each tackled a new and difficult "villain."

4. Before you start, ensure you have an overarching story theme in place.

Great stories have a theme behind them. It is a guide to help with editing and making sure all the parts of your story stay consistent. Every brand should have a theme; they are useful whether you are working on a single execution or planning your initiative pipeline. They can also be used to make better speeches and presentations. This is an exercise I do with teams even if they aren't working on their sequel. You may ask, "What is a theme?" Well, it is what many writers define as the human truth behind your story. The deeper meaning.

Themes are, in effect, the themes of our lives. That's why proverbs, sayings, and common phrases often

> embody themes.[70]
>
> **—Paula Munier**

Here is another great explanation.

> Simply put, a story's theme is its idea or point. The theme of a fable is its moral; the theme of a parable is its teaching; the theme of a story is its view of life.[71]
>
> **—Robert DiYanni, *Literature***

A theme is what your story is really about—the moral of your story. It could be the one thing that you hope your audience will take away or feel if they take away nothing else. When it comes to creating your story, it is the guiding idea. It is not the theme's job to tell the story—it's the story's job to make the theme clear.

Remember that a plot is *what happens*, and a story is what the characters feel and do because of *what happens*. Well, a theme would be a truth about life that emerges from the hero (and audience) experiencing *what happens*.

Themes include many of the pithy-sounding quotes that people use to teach their kids or place at the end of their email signatures. For example, "Slow and steady wins the race," and "Beauty is in the eye of the beholder." A great theme encompasses many facets of human life—that is why it is a human truth.

"Slow and steady wins the race" could be the lesson for a marathon runner, a company making a systemic organizational change, or a painter working on a massive mural.

Themes should never use details that focus solely on a single idea, category, or product. "To provide shareholders better returns through less advertising spending" is *not* a theme. But, "a penny saved is a penny earned" could be.

There are no business acronyms in themes, no chemical ingredients, and no technological descriptions. There are no business words, names, or processes. There are no brand names in a theme. The best themes are timeless human truths like "Don't judge a book by its cover."

Let me explain theme through a film example that I am sure most of you are familiar with, the James Cameron film *Titanic.* Let me ask you, when you saw it, did you wonder if the ship was going to make it? Probably not. So, you knew the ending and you still went to see it. Why? Simple, the great characters and the powerful story. You wanted to see what people would do (specifically the main characters) when faced with that kind of terrifying situation.

So, what do you think *Titanic* is really about? What is the real moral to the story? There are actually a few, but in my opinion, there is one main theme and the others really help support it.

I believe the theme for *Titanic* is "Live the life you want to live." In other words, take control of your life.

Rose is a character who, in the beginning, has no control over her life. Her mother is forcing her to marry a jerk for money so that the mother won't have to work again. Then Rose meets Jack, and Jack has control of his life. He enjoys what he does, and he has no money. This intrigues Rose.

She invites him to dinner one night and the mother is her usual self. She starts asking Jack how someone like him could be on a ship as grand as the Titanic. He says that is why he loves life—you never know what is going to happen, and you can't take anything for granted. Jack goes on to explain that you have to make every day count. This inspires Rose (and most of the people at the table). He also repeats the line "make it count" to Rose later in the film.

At the end of the story, when Rose is an old woman and you see the many pictures from her trips and adventures, you see that she lived life to the fullest and made every day count.[72]

When I go back and watch that film again, it is hard to find a scene that doesn't help move that thematic idea forward in some way. That's what a great theme can do, and it's a great lesson for all of us to remember. Live the life you want to live.

Themes can act as editing tools and ensure that your story doesn't get lost in too many messages or subplots. If you can't explain how each scene (or product) contributes to the larger idea, then it should most likely be cut.

What is *The Godfather* really about? Family and how being in one isn't always easy. What is *Jaws* about? Trust and how an outsider may have to work extra hard to get people to believe what he says. What is *The Shawshank Redemption* about? That life isn't fair: "Get busy living or get busy dying." What is *Star Wars* about? A celebration of friendship and hope. What is the *Wizard of Oz* about? That there is "no place like home."

Most great films have a clear and powerful theme. Great themes are automatically long-lasting because they are usually age-old human truths.

What is your brand's theme?

What are you truly about?

Confidence? Strength? Dependability? Peace of mind? Overcoming challenges? Once you know your truth, then you can use it as an editing tool to make sure your messages, online copy, print campaigns, TV ads, internal conversations, product technologies, packaging, etc. contribute to that. Anything that doesn't support or communicate your theme should be *cut*. It will be a distraction from your larger story or dilute the true power of your message.

A friend once sent me a link to an article about the one-word themes of movies by Christopher Nolan (screenwriter and director of the *Dark Knight* trilogy). According to the article, the themes for each of the Batman films could be summed up in a single word: fear, chaos, and pain, respectively,[73] as Batman begins, falls, and rises. Fantastic! What a simple yet profound look at the moral underpinnings of those films.

This is a great example of the theme being used as a planning vehicle for a larger story line.

The Jason Bourne films have a few themes, but one of them is personal rights versus public safety—unregulated surveillance at the expense of trying to protect everyone. That is definitely a subject matter that is relevant today and a hard dilemma to resolve, as there is both good and bad on either side of the coin (i.e., dilemma).

Below are my interpretations of important themes from some of my other favorite films. I think you will see that they are all common lessons and phrases that apply across many different facets of life.

- "Love is a willingness to sacrifice." – *The Hunger Games*

- "There is no greater warrior than a mother protecting her child." – *Aliens*

- "Even the smallest things can have the biggest impact." – *Lord of the Rings*

- "The whole is greater than the sum of its parts." – *The Avengers*

A good theme is *not* a sell line or tag line. If your theme would look good on a package or print ad, then it is probably *not* a theme. A theme can help you ensure that a single execution maintains your brand message along with helping you plan for future initiatives and ensuring brand consistency. It is a great tool to help you focus on what you really want to stand for. Let's create a quick one for your brand.

Quick exercise: Create your brand theme

Common Theme Buckets

Change versus Tradition	Nature	Technology
Chaos and Order	Necessity of Work	Vanity as Downfall
Dangers of Ignorance	Optimism	Vulnerability
Empowerment	Power of Tradition	Will to Survive
Fear of Failure	Quest for Discovery	Wisdom of Experience
Fulfillment	Coming of Age	Beauty
Inner versus Outer Strength	Self-Awareness	Rebirth

I am including a visual called "Common Theme Buckets" that has various theme directions that your brand story could consider. Is your brand about optimism, empowerment, or maybe self-awareness?

This is in *no way* an exhaustive list, and you can find many more online (such as Grace Fleming's "10 Common Themes in Literature").[74] These are just some of my favorites and a great place to start.

Once you decide on a theme bucket for your story, here is a little trick. Go to Google and type in "quotes about (whatever your theme bucket is)" and then click "images." Let's say you decide your brand is about "empowerment." Go to Google, type in "quotes about empowerment," hit "search," and then hit "images." Look at all the great quotes about empowerment. Now find the one that best matches what your brand is about. Maybe you selected:

> You get in life what you have the courage to ask for.[75]

Write that down. All your executions and messages should help bring that idea to life. Use that theme as a guide as you plan your future "sequels." If the above example were your theme, I would say your brand is about creating courage and helping your consumer feel confident to challenge the way things are done. I would say it must be bold in how it talks and not be afraid to take risks. You get the idea.

So, there you go. A few starting principles to think about and an exercise that I do with teams for both individual projects and for sequel planning sessions.

One of the best sequel plans I have ever seen is what Kevin Feige, Disney, and the Marvel team have put together: a set of films that are all interconnected and all building to a larger whole. It is called the Marvel Cinematic Universe. It is a study in brand management and long-term story planning. That is our next chapter.

WORKBOOK

Chapter Ten Questions

Question: What has been the most powerful "villain" (problem) your brand has dealt with? What was the solution? What is the next villain you will face? How does it raise the emotional stakes of your brand story?

____

____

____

____

____

____

____

____

____

Question: What is the *theme* behind your brand? What quote, saying, or parable communicates that theme best?

Chapter Ten Notes

CHAPTER ELEVEN

Building a Brand's Cinematic Universe

Great sequel strategies have patience built in, which is probably the hardest thing to do. The ability to wait and see the entire story play out, to not rush or move projects because of your competition, to not be reactive but instead remain proactive, to not give into knee-jerk reactions based on fear, to stay the course, is tough to sustain. Yet, that persistence has made all the difference in how powerful the Marvel Cinematic Universe has become for Disney (search the internet for "MCU" and you'll quickly get a sense of its vastness).

I have been consistently blown away at the depth, detail, and links that Marvel (Disney) has created across their films. Look at how many Marvel brands have been brought to life over the last eight years: *Iron Man, The Incredible Hulk, Thor, Captain America, Dr. Strange, Guardians of the Galaxy, Ant-*

Man, Black Panther—and we still have more to go.

Here is the best part, though: all of those stories are connected to one larger story line, the "Infinity Wars" and the arch-villain Thanos (whom so far we have only seen in a couple of "post-credits" scenes and a small bit in *Guardians of the Galaxy*). The amount of detail that Marvel has layered into their stories, ensuring that they all link, that characters and plots feed into one another (even across completely different movies and characters), is amazing.

To do this kind of larger narrative, you have to have what I call a "Map Master," someone who can keep the plan in place across multiple "brands." A map master manages the incredible complexity of each moving part by governing and controlling the hard and soft points of the many different brands. Map masters understand how to provide flexibility to each of the brands' directors while ensuring that each plays their part in building the larger story. They understand the larger story in incredible detail and how all the small pieces fit into the whole.

For Marvel, his name is Kevin Feige, the president of Marvel Studios. I'll bet he has a giant map somewhere in his office that lays out all the connections, both big and small. A detailed web of how everything is linked and is building up to a climactic set of films.

The first *Iron Man* film in 2008 not only got us into the "universe" and introduced Tony Stark, but it also introduced us to Agent Coulson of SHIELD

(Strategic Homeland Intervention, Enforcement, and Logistics Division), Nick Fury (the creator of the Avengers program), and Tony Stark's friend James Rhodes (who later would become War Machine). Amazingly, the "post-credits scene" of this movie also set up the first *Avengers* film.

Agent Coulson would be in multiple films to help Fury assemble the Avengers and would also help kick off the TV series *Agents of SHIELD*. Fury would also be in multiple Marvel films, help bring all the Marvel characters together, and act as a mentor and even a fellow fighter in *Winter Soldier*. "Rhodey" would be in all three *Iron Man* films and also in *Captain America: Civil War*. The *Incredible Hulk* introduced a couple of important things: one, the superhero serum that in the past made Captain America, and two, General Ross, who would show up eight years later in *Captain America: Civil War* to lead the Sokovia Accords.

In *Captain America: Winter Soldier,* a SHIELD agent named Jasper Sitwell (who was really a Hydra agent who briefly appeared in the first *Thor* film and the first *Avengers* film) explained how HYDRA (the "bad guys") planned to eliminate anyone who could pose a threat and threw out a handful of names that were on their list, one of them being Stephen Strange.

That is a 2014 mention of Dr. Strange, who was still a completely unknown character in the film series at that point and who wouldn't have a movie until late 2016.

Amazing planning, and that is just a tiny snapshot of the hundreds of connections that exist. They even have connections between the Netflix series they are doing (such as *Daredevil*, *Luke Cage*, and so on) and the films!

Daredevil takes place in Hell's Kitchen, and his key nemesis is The Kingpin (a mob boss criminal who is making money from his construction companies that are cleaning up NYC after the alien attack in *The Avengers* movie). Sometimes the connections are minor while other times they are more significant. Point being, everyone respects both the previous and future stories.

It's really impressive to see this strategy actually visualized. Google "Marvel Cinematic Universe Maps" to see several examples. My favorite one by far was developed by a designer named Christian Tate; I have included the picture (his site is christiantate.co.uk, Avengers Assembled: Mapping the web of the Marvel Cinematic Universe). It was originally done for Empire Magazine and then updated for British GQ. Thanks again to Christian for letting me share it!

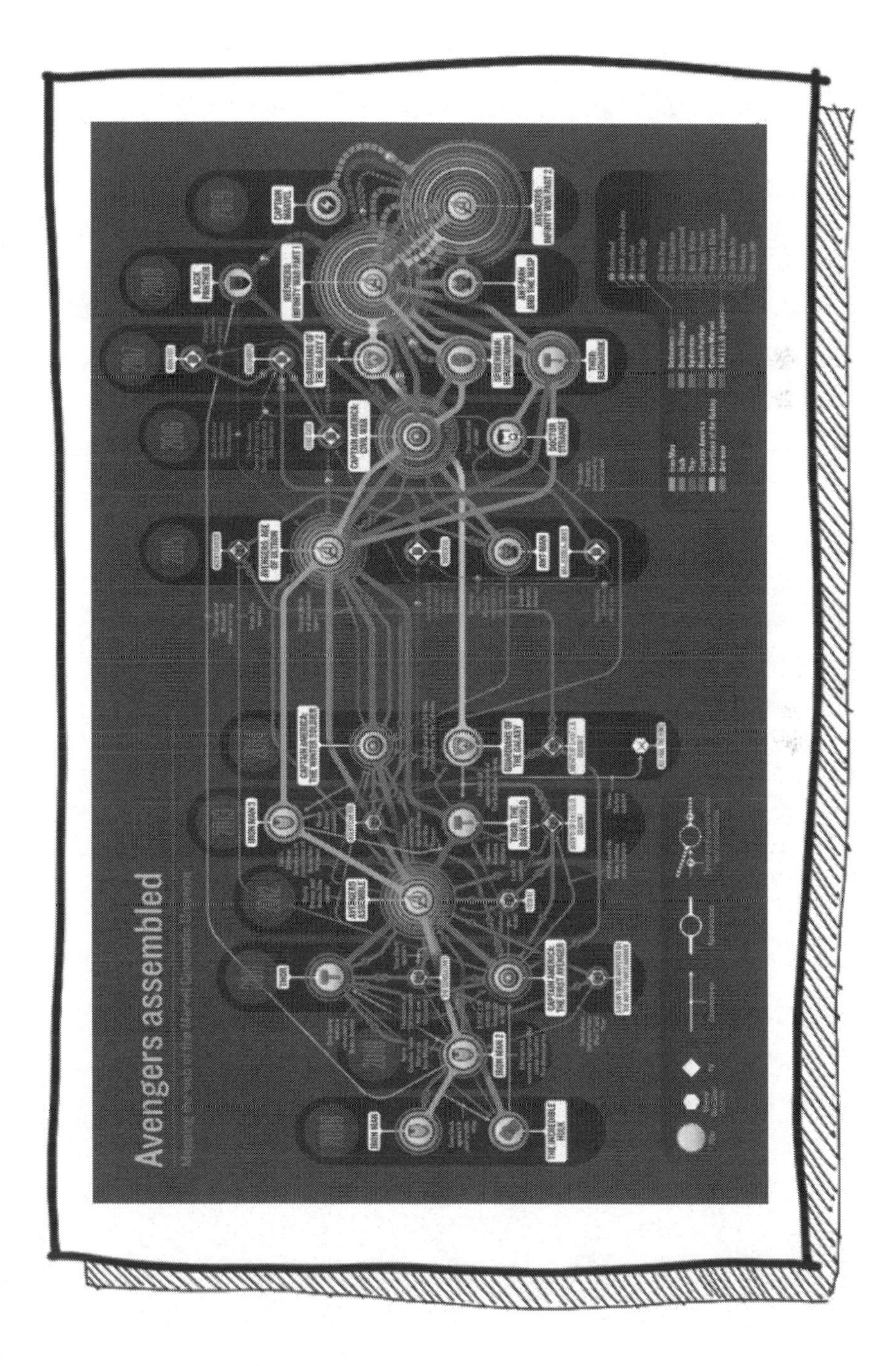
Avengers assembled

The larger "tentpole" films are essentially marked by the multiple big concentric circles.[76] Look at all the intricate connections! Lots of planning and almost ten years' worth of story! Trust me when I say that Marvel is a master class in brand strategy and deployment and worth a close study. There is a lot you can reapply from this kind of thinking. Make a map of your brand's plan.

A story-led masterplan

The key in their approach is that *all* of the connections, small and large, are in service to the greater Marvel storyline, which is leading to the Infinity War and Thanos collecting the mysterious six Infinity Stones to alter the universe. The stones have been showing up separately in different films—the first stone was the Tesseract in *Captain America: The First Avenger* movie and *The Avengers*; the second was the Aether in *Thor: The Dark World*; and so on.

Kevin and his team have such patience and dedication to their plan. For a brand, I believe this could be the ultimate differentiating factor between one that just has an interesting product or technology and one that becomes a household name and part of the social lexicon.

I took you down the Marvel movie path so you could see one of the best story-led masterplans out there. It is also a great place to learn how to take a series of brands or interconnected products and relate them to a larger category or parent brand story. Again, think in terms of "sequels." When they are done well, it will always leave people wanting more. Who wouldn't want that for their brand?

Can you tell me what your brand's larger story really is? How about your story for the next decade? Do all of your employees know it and can they recite it with consistency? Are you willing to launch things not when they are available or based on competitive pressures, but instead when the time is right for your larger story? Do you have multiple teams who are on different projects but are all still linked together as they work on their initiatives? Does everyone know how the smaller brand pieces build into something larger?

If so, BRAVO!

If not, what a great way to think about future planning. This is what a great sequel plan can look like. The Marvel example is the culmination of all the story tools we have discussed. It has a detailed brand story made up of all the story ingredients, a high-level theme (I think the theme across the Marvel films is something like "the needs of the many outweigh the needs of the few"), menacing villains, and a clear sequel strategy for future planning. I call that a Brand Screenplay. Whether or not great brands call it that is not really important; this kind of thinking is what they do, what they have, and what they follow. They have a plan that everyone understands. A guide made up of great stories. A road map. Feige says it best.

> When Tony Stark and Stark Industries and the world of that first movie was the definition of the Cinematic Universe, the question was how do you bring a soldier from WWII into that in a way that makes sense, how do you bring a Norse god from a whole other planet into it, how do you introduce flying aircraft carriers into that? That was the challenge. Now—particularly after *Avengers*, after *Guardians*, after [*Doctor Strange*]—the sky's the limit with where we go.[77]
>
> **—Kevin Feige**

Once the larger plan is set up (which is clearly the hardest part), the resulting brand world becomes a well-established, clear, and detailed playground. But don't fear: it can still offer a ton of flexibility.

Many of the Marvel films had different directors and teams, and each was able to put their personal style and ideas into it. Every director was still able to add their secret spice.

For that to work, there needs to be definite hard and soft points, and anyone working on it has to understand and adhere to those.

Here is another quote from Feige to explain how Ryan Coogler, *Black Panther*'s director, would have to build into the larger story but would also have some freedom on how to bring his specific film to life.

> Each *Avengers* film had to feel like they were part of the same whole. At the end of *Civil War*, we show a glimpse at Wakanda. We promised Ryan Coogler we wouldn't show too much, which is why it's so misty at the end. We didn't want to lock him into anything.[78]
>
> **—Kevin Feige**

Do some research on the Marvel approach. You can find a lot of articles on it. I have found it incredibly inspiring. Doing sequel planning is not easy though, so let's talk about a few "watch-outs" to remember:

First, keep raising the bar. Remember, in a story, what is happening now must be more interesting than what just happened. Take things to the next level! Keep moving up!

Second, remember that people know you from your last story. If it was bad, you will have to deal with that and really deliver next time. If it was great, then they will have very high expectations, so be prepared. It is always better that they are anxious for your next "film."

Third, you need a "map master." This could be a team or an individual. Someone to run the larger story plan and keep all the stories straight and working together. You also need a wall to put the plan on! Make it visual. The map master also needs to be given the authority to have *veto* rights on any individual "film" and any execution (call that projects and initiatives). The final call has to stop with them. They also need to be the owner of ensuring that the agreed hard and soft points are being followed correctly. They are a critical figure, and giving them the appropriate authority is essential to the success of your plan.

Fourth, remember that your sequel is only as powerful as the quality of the villain (the obstacle/conflict). A weak problem will usually equal a weak story. I know we have talked about this a couple times, but that is because it is *so* important.

One last piece of advice: *Always* try to think of your sequels like a fan would—what would you want to see? What would get you excited? What would disappoint you? Give yourself some credit. If you know the brand, don't forget to trust your gut.

And, one last quote from Kevin Feige to stress the importance of thinking ahead with your sequel plan.

> I have a belief that if you are lucky enough to get to part three of a franchise, it is your obligation not to fall to threequel-itis.[79]
>
> **—Kevin Feige**

WORKBOOK

Chapter Eleven Questions

Question: Who is your map master and what decision power do they have? Do you have a larger brand story that can be the basis for your sequel plan?

Question: Using that larger brand story, chart out all your initiatives in a meaningful way. What does that story look like over five, ten, or even twenty years? How does each project build into the larger story? Lastly, what are the brand's hard and soft points that everyone on the team needs to understand?

Chapter Eleven Notes

CHAPTER TWELVE

Brand Mythology

You now know what great stories can do, the power they can have, the ingredients that make them up, the structures and bones behind them, and how to use them as a planning tool.

Another way to bring all of this back to your brand is to talk about your Brand Mythology.

The words "myth" and "mythology" are often given a bad reputation. Sometimes people hear these words and instantly think "lie, fake, fairy-tale." But that really isn't true. Myths were truths to the people who created and believed in them. They were the recipes for living; Campbell sometimes called them the "experience of meaning."[80] Myths and the idea of mythology come from a very important part of the human heart and mind—the part that wants and needs explanations to unanswered questions.

Cultures (ancient and present day) have always used mythology to explain things that mystified them. Myths were the answers to a group's biggest questions and were often explained by the leaders, shamans, and town elders. Today that can be brands, company management, CEOs, or visionaries.

Myths and other folklore were based on what people understood at that moment using the tools and experiences they had access to. People believed these truths, they trusted them, and, at that time, they were the best explanations to be found.

If you are out on a boat and look to the horizon, does the world look curved or flat? It looks flat. It wasn't that long ago that we assumed the world was flat simply because that is what our eyes told us.

Isn't it interesting how many things science has "proven" just to "disprove" later? I don't look at past cultures and think of their myths and beliefs as silly, particularly when you think about what they knew at the time.

How would they know the world was round based on what that time period had access to? They made the best guesses they could, given what they could see and understand at that moment.

Therefore, I believe new myths are created every day while old myths evolve or change over time as we learn more. Despite everything scientists believe they know, their knowledge is still incomplete, so, they create new myths for the things they don't know. They, like the cultures of old, must make educated guesses on many ideas based on what they understand at that moment. Those guesses become their truth until proven otherwise.

That's similar to the approach ancient Egyptians used to explain how the big yellow ball in the sky moved each day. They believed there was a giant beetle moving it; they based that idea on a beetle they could see every day moving balls across the sand, the dung beetle. So, it made sense that there might be a big one moving the yellow ball across the desert of the sky.[81] That seemed intuitive and was based on something real they saw every day.

Mythologies are a part of who we are, and a lot of things we know and do are based on mythology. Many holidays and traditions have some grounding in mythology. Similarly, many family customs are also bound in mythology.

The same is true for brands. Brand mythology is company lore—the creation stories, the founding stories, the employee stories, and the company vision stories. It is your purpose and manifesto and reason for being. The best brands always have a strong mythology at their core.

Applying mythology to brands

Years ago, I did a quick internet search on "mythology" and arrived at three basic meanings:

1. **Symbolic** stories that help reconcile the realities of life.[82]
2. **Extraordinary** stories concerning the history of a people or explaining some phenomenon.[83]
3. **Sacred** stories, based upon tradition, that explain the world, an idea, or an experience.[84]

When I share my presentation with project teams, I make a point of stressing the first word of each of those definitions—symbolic, extraordinary, and sacred. Brand stories that are important have these. The Tide invention story I told you in the beginning of the book has all three of these!

A brand mythology is made up of your most powerful stories, symbols, and rituals; and if you want your brand to last, you will need those.

Try this out. Write down what you believe your brand's most powerful stories, symbols, and rituals are.

Brand mythology doesn't necessarily have to be about the product technology; rather, it is about the larger story. One hundred years from now, which of these two brands will be talked about around campfires the most—Starbucks or Folgers? I am a fan of both, but one really sticks out.

Folgers and its "The Best Part of Waking Up" campaign is famous. Each time you saw it, you could almost smell the coffee in those ads. But, let's be honest, Starbucks is the brand that really educated most of the United States about coffee. They taught everyone a whole new language (like "grande, triple, no foam, skinny latte") and opened our eyes to the variety of coffees from around the world. They also showed us new and unique preparation methods, introduced the barista concept, and put a value on the role coffee can play in a social experience (see Howard Schultz's insight on the "Third Place").[85] They helped evolve gas stations into coffee centers and put coffee shops in our grocery stores.

Starbucks wasn't a product, it was a way of thinking and being part of the coffee culture. It was, and still is, a part of our modern-day coffee mythology. It also has a distinctive symbol that everyone knows (does a little green circle with a mermaid in it sound familiar?). Imagine the stories that will be told 500 years from now about the origin of Starbucks. What stories will you tell about it to your great-grandchildren?

It was even influential in a very successful TV series called *Friends* (the coffee shop Central Perk was clearly a representation of the Starbucks "Third Place" idea).[86]

Four key roles for any brand mythology

Let's return to Joseph Campbell to go a step

deeper into mythology. Campbell said that mythologies have four roles to play. There is a *mystical* role, which is about creating wonder, interest, and intrigue; a *cosmological* role, which is about explaining or answering something; a *sociological* role, which is about creating a system and infrastructure within a culture, society, or a person's life; and finally, a *pedagogical* role, which is about being easy to understand, being personal, being human, and being relevant.[87]

I am of course summarizing these four with more of a brand angle in mind, and great brands do all of these well.

As you begin to think about your brand and its mythology, start with these four questions:

1. What really makes your brand stand out, and why is it unique?
2. Why does it exist?
3. How does it fit into people's lives?
4. Why should they care?

In my workshops, I usually explain these four principles using one of my favorite holidays, Thanksgiving. Thanksgiving is a wonderful day to get the family together, have fun, catch up, and celebrate.

So, what is the *Mystical* part of this holiday?

None of us were really around for the first Thanksgiving holiday, particularly the actual event that led to its creation (the Pilgrims coming to the new world). The Pilgrims' journey was a harrowing and amazing tale of leaving their old world behind to go to a new world, full of the unknown in hopes of a better life. Quite the adventure.

The *Cosmological* portion of the holiday answers the question, *why did the Pilgrims do this*? It was for religious freedom. Today the *why* is to "give thanks" for great friends, family, health, and anything else that we see as good fortune in our lives, and to also remember what is truly important.

The *Sociological* part involves the symbols, stories, and rituals that center around Thanksgiving, and there are a lot of them. There is a specific month, a day, a season, icons, color palettes, foods, ceremonies, TV shows, locations—it's all actually

pretty set.

Lastly, how is it *Pedagogical*? Well, it is personal,

human, and easy to understand. The name is "Thanksgiving" or reversed "giving thanks"—that is pretty simple. Each family has their own customs they bring to it. At our Thanksgiving, we don't just have pumpkin pie; we have my grandma's secret recipe pumpkin pie. We also like to play certain games after dinner and some of us watch football.

So here is the amazing thing. Countless people are celebrating the "mythology" of this holiday each year, on the same day, with the same basic structure and rules behind it, but they are also making it uniquely their own!

Mythologies should capture a brand's truth

Let's go back to McKee's definition of story from the beginning. Here it is again.

> Storytelling is the creative demonstration of truth, the living proof of an idea and the conversion of idea to action.[88]
>
> **—Robert McKee**

Now, substitute the word "storytelling" with the words "A great brand..." The definition still holds true, doesn't it? That is how I knew that brands need to have a powerful story, and it starts with understanding or having a mythology.

Your brand is "the creative demonstration of

truth," a truth, your truth, a group's truth that you all believe in. When done well, with insight and consistency, brand mythologies can become legends—and we all know that legends can remain strong through the ages. Legends last.

A brand mythology should be a detailed set of stories and beliefs that you all share; it should be the "why" and the "how" that makes your company unique; it should be the rituals you have and the meanings behind them; it should be your origin and creation story and why those are important. It should not simply be a look back at history (which can appear dated or not useful), but instead a look through history, which can inspire and guide in very meaningful ways. Most importantly, it should be documented, shared, and protected.

For example, at P&G we call ourselves "*Proctoids*." That is because we have a mythology like any strong tribe does. You couldn't just move someone from P&G to another company and expect that they could jump right in and that all the processes and methods would be the same. It would take some time to learn the "rules" for their new tribe.

P&G does things a certain way, they speak a certain language, and they have certain processes and methods that are unique to them. That is why it is Procter & Gamble and not just *any* company. The same goes for *your* company.

Your company is unique. Sometimes you have to look closely to really understand what makes you stand out.

Robert McKee says a business leader should think about their brand as if they were an author.[89] So, like an author, you have to know your "world" better than anyone. I once heard a similar saying in a writing class I took years ago: that an author essentially needs to be the "god" of their literary world and that "not a leaf should fall that they are not aware of." That saying is actually from the fifty-ninth verse of chapter six of the Quran:

> And with Him are the keys of the unseen; none knows them except Him. And He knows what is on the land and in the sea. Not a leaf falls but that He knows it.[90]

You need to understand the rules of your world and everything behind it—you are one of its creators. So, metaphorically speaking, "not a leaf should fall" in your company or on your brand that you and your colleagues do not know about and understand why. Trust me, Kevin Feige knows every leaf that falls in the Marvel Cinematic Universe. Does your management?

Principles for creating brand mythology

Spend some time conducting employee interviews at your company to get a snapshot of how people are feeling about their work, their team, and the company in general. Interviews and the stories that come from them are one of the best ways to understand your mythology and company culture. They can also help shine a spotlight on things that aren't working and need to be addressed. These need to be done one-on-one. Please, no surveys. Those are too impersonal and don't get at the real issues.

When you do the one-on-one, ask people to bring three pictures with them to the discussion: one that represents the culture of the company's "past," one for the "present," and one for what they believe will be the "future" given the current direction. Go through each in detail with them. A picture is worth a thousand words, right? Do about twenty to thirty of these across different levels and in different departments, and then put together a *company story* report with a collage of the pictures and the insights you heard. Share it with management. This is a great way to start to understand what your company story really is at that moment.

I believe there are five important principles in developing a strong brand mythology. Even if you are just starting your company or brand, consider these five and be very deliberate about creating them.

1. Identify what is story-worthy.

The first brand mythology principle is understanding what is truly story-worthy about your company and your products. Whatever you make, whatever your service or idea, saying that you believe in "high-quality products" or "good people" or "doing the right thing" is not very story worthy. Why? Because what company doesn't want or already believe in those things?

Again, as we have said before, that is a choice between a positive and a negative, so therefore it's not much of a choice at all. Those are all a point of entry for any good company today. What is it that you do or believe in that truly makes your company and brand stand out from the rest? Why should people talk about you with their friends while they are out at a bar some Friday? If you had to pick one key thing that truly sets you apart from your competition, what would that be?

Walt Disney World doesn't say "we have rides like other parks." Any theme park or amusement park has rides. At Disney, they talk about magic and fantasy, memorable family moments, lovable characters, amazing attention to detail, immersive storytelling, and your whole family being kids again. They create and love to deliver "magic moments," just as the janitor did for my friend Steve.

Try to avoid business buzzwords! "Innovation" is a common one—sorry, not story worthy! It's what you do with that word or the unique approach that your company takes to innovation that could be unique.

When you see corporate lingo being used, just ask yourself this question: "What will someone do differently in their job today now that I have shared this word with them?"

If you don't get a specific answer, then it probably was not helpful. That is why "innovation" by itself doesn't work. Everyone in your company should already assume they have to do that. There is a big difference between a reminder and a challenge.

If you have to use buzzwords, make sure you at least expand on them and add some kind of inspiring details to make them personal. In his book *All Marketers Tell Stories: The Power of Telling Authentic Stories in a Low Trust World,* Seth Godin writes, *"Either you are going to tell stories that spread, or you will become irrelevant. No one buys features, they buy the story."*[91]

Brand features are easily copied and quick to become the category status quo, but stories about them can last and set you apart.

2. Be consistent with your expressions.

The second principle of a brand mythology is *consistency*. Picture a person who works in a Harley-Davidson factory making bikes or someone who loves to ride a Harley. Got a picture in your head? Now go to their website and look at the pictures there. Were you close? I'll bet you were. Harley-Davidson is a wonderful "character" brand and very consistently executed.

There is almost a set of rules that we all seem to know on how to dress, look, talk, and act to be part of that brand. The hard and soft points again.

Harley-Davidson also has a rich history that is part of their company story. The logo, color palette, tone of voice, language, photography style, and the product itself all support their story and are handled very consistently. All the brand touch points fit together and build to that larger story: rebellion, freedom, the open road, and camaraderie.

Harley-Davidson is what I call a "Clark Kent"

brand. It allows you to jump into a phone booth, become a different character for a short period, and then go back to your other persona.

I had a good friend some years ago who fit this perfectly. By day, he was a brilliant mechanical engineer who wore the company standard dress pants and dress shirt with a tie. He was clean-shaven and soft-spoken, but on the weekend he unlocked an entirely different persona! When he and his friends got out their Harleys, they put on their biker outfits and set out on the open road with the powerful rumble following them wherever they went. Then on Monday, all was back to normal, and he was a mechanical engineer again at a Dow 30 company (I miss you Marty!).

Harley also creates journeys and events where their riders can meet, talk, and trade stories. They capture rider stories to add to their brand mythology. They focus on the riders' experiences, their hero's journey.

With the rise of the digital age and Millennials, they will now have to decide how to translate all of this into very new media with new potential consumers, but I am confident they will. They have always been very dedicated to having a great story and understanding what their *who* really wants.

Mythologies need to stay true to themselves. Mexico still uses one of their mythological icons all across their country—on both their flag and their currency. The eagle with a snake in its talons sitting atop a cactus is a symbol of foundation and of civilization. It is a symbol that the Aztecs looked for to decide where to build their great city, which is why Mexico City is in its current location.

3. Identify powerful brand stories, symbols, and rituals.

The third principle of brand mythology involves

your brand's stories, symbols, and rituals. We have talked about these already, and one of my favorite examples is Tiffany. Isn't it amazing the emotional power a blue cardboard box with a small white ribbon can have?

Tiffany is such a great brand, and it's one of the most prestigious brands out there. They have a long heritage with a rich tapestry of emotional moments and consumer narratives to back up their story.

Tell me this: what are Tiffany brand stories usually about? What kind of personal moment is Tiffany usually a part of?

Now, ask a friend those same questions and see how similar the answers are. I think you will find that they are usually pretty consistent. Just ask someone if they have ever received a "blue box" for Christmas or Valentine's Day. Did they know what you were talking about? Probably.

So, the color itself—"Tiffany Blue"—is one of their primary symbols. Then there is the iconic Tiffany Blue Box, which is secured delicately with a white ribbon.[92] Wherever you are in the world, if you go into a Tiffany's, you will get the same blue box wrapped with a white ribbon in the same way.

Then they have a photography style, print ads, store design, and are also known for their beautiful holiday window displays. They are even associated with a movie, *Breakfast at Tiffany's*.

What about their rituals? They have several they design for and showcase. Proposals, anniversaries, birthdays, Valentine's Day, and Christmas are a few of the big ones. They also focus on romantic moments. They don't really go after Halloween, Easter, the Fourth of July, or St. Patrick's Day.

Someone in one of my sessions a while ago said they also are great for "I'm sorry" moments (although if you have to go to Tiffany's to say "sorry," then you've really messed up).

If just your box, color, and name can bring that kind of excitement to your customers, across generations, then you have a great set of stories, symbols, and rituals.

Now, take a moment to write down the following for your brand:

- What are your best stories? (origin, key innovations, influential employees, powerful experiences, key leaders, etc.)
- What are your symbols? (What are you known for—if people had to describe your brand, what would be the first asset they would talk about?)
- What are your rituals? (Where or how is your brand/product used? What are the key moments where you show up? What specific situations make you not only relevant but also important?)

How did you do? How does your brand look? Now, do the same for your competition. Compare the two and be honest. Where do you stand out? What things about your competition look *truly* different from yours? Are they better? Is there anything that is too similar? If there is, you may still have work to do.

Make sure that when you answer the questions above that you are answering from the consumer's (your hero's) perspective. Not yours. If you think your color is a key asset but no consumer describes it that way, then you are talking to yourself.

4. Tell your story first, and then bring up data.

We really need to talk this one in detail: brands and businesses need data. It is a critical part of business and for good reason. Data aids in key measures. Data guides important choices and can help set goals. But be careful, as it sometimes has a certain addictive quality to it that can quickly move it from helpful to harmful.

Data can become a crutch or be seen as "the answer." It can make you lose sight of the fact that people are human beings, not just numbers.

Moreover, human beings are simply not data-driven creatures. We are impulsive, emotional, and irrational. In many cases, we use data more retroactively to justify what we do versus using it proactively.

Consider this for a moment. Data indicating that if we eat well and exercise we will most likely live longer has been shared with folks since they were children. But does everyone do that? Does this country have health problems because of the lack of exercise and poor diet? Will people even tell you that they know they should eat better and exercise but still don't?

We have been told over and over, and even shown the hard data, that you will live *longer* with simple habit changes! We even know exactly what to stop doing and what to start doing! And yet many simply don't do it.

In a recent ad campaign to promote the work of a Swedish nonprofit company, Stephen Hawking said, "For what it's worth, how being sedentary has been a major health problem is beyond my understanding. Today too many people die from complications related to overweight and obesity. We eat too much and move too little. It's not rocket science."[93]

Data has also shown that smoking is bad for you. It is backed by a lot of science and research, but has the world stopped doing it? You will literally hear smokers say that they know they should quit.

I just read online that one alcoholic drink a day can potentially have some health benefits to it, but anything more than one and the benefits start to decline quickly. Beer has antioxidants, can help reduce the risk of diabetes, and lowers the risk of gallstones; but too much of it is also very hard on your liver and may cause brain damage.[94] Now that I know that, I guess I should stop after that first beer this Friday. If I am really honest: I won't. I love beer, especially craft ones. I usually have more than one. Well, there goes the health benefits.

Both political parties have lots of data. Do they both see themselves as right? Sure they do! Remember, truth is subjective. It always comes down to what you believe (or want to believe).

Remember McKee's definition of a story? A "truth," your truth, your personal truth. What *you* believe. If the numbers don't fit your story, then you won't do much with them. If you want numbers to matter, then you better find an emotional way to connect them with the audience.

> Stories anchor our beliefs. If you have a story, the only thing that will change your mind is a better story.[95]
>
> **—Daniel Taylor, *The Healing Power of Stories***

Data alone doesn't often change someone's story beliefs. To do that, you simply may need a better story.

The next time you are in an argument with your significant other, try to use data as your argument point and be sure to call it that. Why not put your argument at home into a PowerPoint deck like you do at work?

Have you ever been on a roller coaster (or any other thrill ride)? I'm sure you have. So, please, explain to me the role a roller coaster plays in species survival?

It's really pretty silly, isn't it? You are willing to get on a machine that you didn't get to see built or maintained, that you will pay to ride, wait in a line for, let a sixteen-year-old strap you into, and then zoom around curves at high speed, all so you can do one simple thing—scream and have fun. How very logical you are. You also may take your bloodline on with you! The reality is it's an unnecessary risk. You are doing it purely for emotion, and I love them and ride them every year with my kids!

We are human beings and we like to feel emotions, have experiences, try new things, eat tasty food, and enjoy life. We want to live. We also are very short-term-thinking creatures; we are far more likely to look to tomorrow before we look twenty years from now. It's a lot easier to live for the day than to prepare for a future that you don't know will ever arrive. That is one reason why the majority of the country hasn't saved nearly as much as they should have for retirement.

Remember that your consumers aren't numbers. They aren't computer algorithms; they are people with emotions, with families, with good and bad days, with joy, with struggles and tragedy, with passions. They want to live life to the fullest, just like you.

Presenting data in the wrong way can even sound like you are calling the other person "stupid," which is also not a good strategy. Aristotle once said something along these lines: to convince people, you need to use intellect, emotion, and charisma (he called them *logos*, *pathos*, and *ethos*).[96] You need all three. That is as true today as it was then.

The legend of the "Hemingway Challenge" demonstrates the power of pathos. As the story goes, Ernest Hemingway once took a bet to write a story in only six words.[97] The poignancy of the half dozen words he chose (I will share them later) emphasizes the strength of our basic human urge to invest emotionally into even the simplest narrative.

The best brands understand you need both head *and* heart, not head *or* heart. Your brand mythology can't be all facts and numbers. To be truly story-worthy, symbols and rituals require strong emotion.

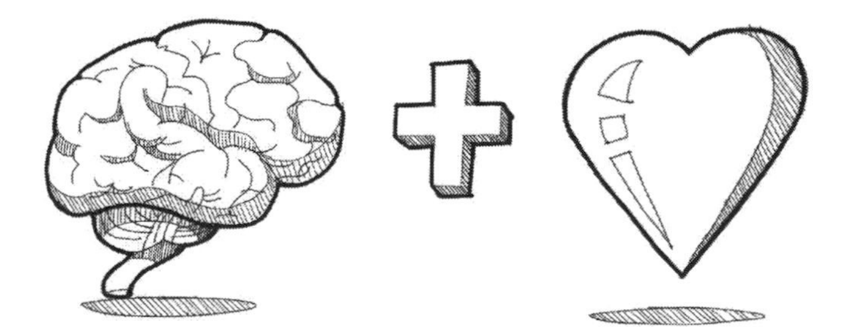

Amazon has a great blend of head and heart stories that accompany each product. They are called "reviews." People are willing to spend a lot of money based on a bunch of "first name only" individuals, the number of gold stars they award the product, and the stories they share—gold stars provided from someone you don't even know.

Remember when you were a kid and you got a gold star? What words were written next to those stars? "Good Job" or "Great Work," right? Who wouldn't want to buy a 4.4 gold star product instead of the 2.3 one, especially since "Pat from Boise" and "Tom from Nashville" both agree it's great? Well done, I say!

Most reviews on Amazon are told like stories. The consumer explains the treasure they were after, the struggles they went through, the hard decisions they made, the research they did, the insights they discovered, and in the end, the lesson or epiphany they found. They don't include data sheets, lots of pie charts and graphs—they tell stories.

Emotion, subjective interpretation, gut, and passion will always come into play, even during your most "data driven" decisions.

Story + Data can be very powerful. Just don't lose the emotion that is behind the numbers. Whether you're a new hire or a manager, the only reason a number really has any power is because it triggers some kind of feeling in you...fear, dread, excitement, or maybe joy.

When you must present data, don't lose the passion. Don't lose the insight or your perspective on what you think it means. If a company only wanted data, they wouldn't need people. They could just let computers do most of that work. It is what YOU bring to the data that can really make it come to life.

I hope you remember what happened in the movie *The Terminator.* You leave things up to the computers and the numbers, and eventually humans are seen as part of the problem.

According to Jennifer Aaker, a social psychologist from Stanford Graduate School of Business, research shows that "stories are remembered up to twenty-two times more than facts alone."[98]

Along similar lines, an experiment was conducted by Deborah Small, George Lowenstein, and Paul Slovic at Carnegie Mellon University that centered around the idea of empathy for identifiable victims.

Basically, the team wanted to examine the role that story and data played in donation situations and how it would affect the total amount given. The subject matter used was how poverty in rural Africa was affecting children. They had three different tests: one with just the data and facts about the children, one with data and a small amount of story, and one that was a story about a girl named Rokia. Her story had a picture of her and this short paragraph:

> Rokia, a seven-year-old girl from Mali, Africa, is desperately poor and faces a threat of severe hunger or even starvation. Her life will be changed for the better as a result of your financial gift. With your support, and

> the support of other caring sponsors, Save the Children will work with Rokia's family and other members of the community to help feed her and provide her with education, as well as basic medical care and hygiene education.[99]

When just the data was shared, the average donation was $1.14. When there was data and a small amount of story, the donation increased to $1.43. But when the Rokia story was shared, the donation jumped to $2.43.

Researchers quickly found that people relate to faces, not numbers. Makes sense, doesn't it? Mother Teresa once said, *"If I look at the mass I will never act. If I look at the one, I will."*[100]

Now, I want to stress that I'm not saying to avoid data. Quite the contrary, it can be very powerful, but you should first start with a great story and then let the numbers help bring it life. The emotion gets you hooked and data can help support it.

> People hear statistics, but they feel stories.[101]

5. Build a strong company and brand culture.

The last principle in brand mythology is "Culture." I always save this one for last because it really is the most important. Hopefully, you have heard the old saying "*Culture Eats Strategy for Breakfast.*"

This should be plastered on the walls in office buildings as a constant reminder that your actions always speak louder than words.

You can share all the company mission statements, beliefs documents, and manifestos you want, but if there aren't stories to back those up, they won't mean much. Without stories, they become a bunch of fancy words with no real evidence or proof.

Your company stories can help shape and influence the culture that you want to have (it can also work in reverse and move you away from the culture you want). Remember the David Byerly and Tide story? That is a perfect example of how a story can have a very positive cultural effect.

Do you have a group struggling with an innovation project? Share a story like that and remind them that failing is part of innovating, and that nothing worthwhile is easy. Stress the importance of tenacity. Or maybe you have a manager who wants his team to have at least one personal project on their roster. Tell that same story but this time from David's manager's perspective. Remind them that a great manager is there to stand behind their employees and provide the support needed to do the work along with letting them explore their own ideas.

To me, a company's culture can only be defined by one thing—the stories that the employees love, share, and tell. Employee stories will tell you the real organizational health of your company—they are the company heartbeat and spirit.

I presented my story content several years ago at Columbia Sportswear, a great brand and a great group of people. They also own one of my favorite camping brands, Mountain Hardwear. As an avid backpacker and camper, I was really excited to present to their team.

I quickly learned just how much they loved the outdoors and the products they designed, and it is one of my favorite culture stories to share.

So, the design team at Columbia was having their team offsite at a place called Redmond, Oregon. Redmond is a beautiful, small city a few hours' drive from Portland. The meeting location was going to be at a ranch outside of town. This ranch had cabins for everyone to stay in.

I arrived and asked my contact which cabin I should put my stuff in (the team was already there, so I assumed that most would be full). He quickly replied that there were plenty of them open since a lot of people didn't use them.

"What?" I said.

He gestured to the far end of the complex, where there were a bunch of tents set up.

He then explained that a large group of the team had brought tents and wanted to sleep in those, including some of the management!

So, a huge group of employees gave up sleeping

in cabins so they could sleep in tents at their company offsite meeting. Now, do I know how much they love the outdoors? I sure do, and I have been loyal to their products ever since!

What story would you tell me to demonstrate how much *you* and your company love what you do? What story would you share that would make clear the mission your company is on? Those are the stories that can truly help influence and inspire a great culture.

Blake Mycoskie of TOMS Shoes said it well:

> I realized the importance of having a story today is what really separates companies. People don't just wear our shoes, they tell our story.[102]
>
> **—Blake Mycoskie**

Another great culture story example is the company REI, another outdoor brand that is passionate about what they do. They took a stand a couple of years ago to not only be closed on Thanksgiving (which is becoming more and more rare), but to also be closed on Black Friday. They called it their #OptOutside movement.

They skipped one of the biggest shopping days of the year and in doing so showed that their company values family time and being outside together.

A decision like that is a great example of a story dilemma because it's not just the choice between a positive and a negative. There is a sacrifice being made, and, with that, real stakes are being put in the ground.

Stories like this show they are a business with strong principles that they are willing to stand by. They walk the talk and people recognize it.

Just go online and look at some of the wonderful consumer comments after their Black Friday campaign. They also became an inspiration for many other companies to make a similar stand. Like I said, tell a great story and people always find the time to hear it.

What do the companies who open earlier and earlier on Thanksgiving believe in if they insist on asking their employees to leave family and friends that day? What is most important to them?

The culture at Walt Disney is another classic example. Most people who have been to Disney have at least one great family story where there was some kind of "magical moment" and how Disney went above and beyond what was expected.

I remember not too many years ago, my mom and stepdad took us to Walt Disney World (my wife, all three of our kids, and me). It was one of my favorite vacations of all time. I remember how I felt the last day we were there, and I admit that I was pretty teary-eyed.

It was one of the most magical trips we had ever been on. To this day, almost nine years later, we still talk about it. My kids were in a constant state of joy the whole time, and everything in the entire experience just clicked. Disney had helped organize everything for us—great meals, fun tours, and special events. We were consistently impressed by the little extras Disney would provide; for example, housekeeping made fun little animals out of our room towels each morning.

One night, we watched the fireworks from a boat in the Seven Seas Lagoon, and Peter Pan was there at the end to greet everyone (the boat launched after meeting Captain Hook). My kids had fallen asleep—they were totally pooped out—but we knew they would want their picture with Peter Pan.

As we were discussing if we should wake them, the character came up to us and said he would be happy to take a picture with us just holding our sleeping kids (which ended up being a really cute picture, by the way). People at Disney World just love what they do and it shows.

I went there once as part of a corporate offsite and had an afternoon free, so I took one of the behind-the-scenes tours at the Magic Kingdom. I loved it and highly recommend it!

Afterward, I was talking to the guide, who was a retired history teacher and loved to tell stories. He said that as soon as he retired he decided he wanted to be a tour guide at Walt Disney World and he had been doing it for over ten years. He loved seeing the smiles on people's faces when he gave them a small peek behind the curtain. It sounds like a lot of fun to me too!

As a Disney fanatic, when I was asked to present my story content to them a few years ago, it was truly a career highlight. Then they even had me back to present a second time! I will never forget it!

The first time was at a TED-style offsite with both internal and external speakers. I was very excited (and also nervous)!

One of the other presenters was none other than Glen Keane, the world-famous artist and character artist behind characters like Ariel from *The Little Mermaid* and the Beast from *Beauty and the Beast* (he worked on many more, too)!

After my pres-entation, there was a short break and he and I chatted briefly. As he was asking a couple of questions about my content, he pulled out his notebook and flipped to the page with his notes. I immediately noticed something—he had a drawing of me on it!

I remember thinking, "Glen Keane took notes from my talk and actually sketched me!" I asked if I could take a picture of the drawing and he said sure.

At a cocktail party later, he came up to me and said that if I would send him the picture I took (since it had the notes on it), he would give me the actual drawing. I sent the picture to him that second and he wrote a nice little note on the drawing, signed it, tore it out, and gave it to me. Now I have a drawing of me done by Glen Keane. Talk about a "magic moment."

You know I love *Star Wars*. Well, not long ago I was asked to speak at a conference in San Francisco and of course the Lucasfilm offices are in town. Before I left for the trip, I contacted my friend at Disney to see if she knew anyone there who may be willing to give me a brief tour—even for just fifteen minutes. She said she would send a note to some friends there and see what she could do.

Sure enough, the weekend before I left, she called me at home to tell me that two wonderful Lucasfilm employees would be happy to show me around. The rest is history as I got a two-hour private tour of their facilities (thanks again, Libby)!

Amazing things like this happen at Disney every

day. It is simply who and what they are.

What kind of events and stories do you want to be the norm at your company? You have to plan for those, share them, celebrate them, and be *very* specific on what they are.

Be careful though. Culture is not a "project"; it is a way of being, of behaving, and it is organic, living, and breathing. Many people will say culture is the "look and smell of a place." That you can tell what it is right when you walk in and see the people, their desks, how they are dressed, how they interact, and how they behave. It will grow on its own and happen with or without you trying to build it. It is not a checklist item or something you can create through a single initiative. It is not something you can understand from a survey. A great culture takes years of consistent behavior, dedication, and great storytelling. You cannot just say "We have decided that our culture will be more (*fill in the blank*)." That doesn't work. You have to let it grow, be patient, and nurture it with the right behaviors and stories.

Find, share, and protect the stories that you need within your company. This is why a company archive and a heritage center are so important! A story not told is a wasted story. A well-managed archive is a goldmine for insights. As we say at P&G, *"No company can afford the luxury of rediscovering its own prior knowledge."*

Well, there you go. Call all that we have covered a bit of Story 101. In my next book, I plan to go deeper into many of these specific chapters and share more tools and some case studies. My intent with this one was to just give a good starting story foundation to hopefully get you thinking about the power a story can have. Remember, this is just my personal perspective. Check out the many, many other books out there! There are so many great story resources, with examples across all industries. Build a story library at home and start to fill it with books, articles, examples...take classes...watch movies...do lots of research!

I don't want to leave, though, without sharing a few tools I use with teams in my workshops. Let's explore a little Story 201. That will be the rest of this book.

WORKBOOK

Chapter Twelve Questions

Question: What are the key stories, symbols, and rituals associated with your brand or company?

Question: How do you capture those, and how are they being protected and shared?

____

____

____

____

____

____

____

____

____

____

____

____

Chapter Twelve Notes

CHAPTER THIRTEEN

A Simple Story-Writing Structure

What are some helpful tools to use when it is time to create your story? The principles we have talked about are a good start, but you eventually need to sit down and do some writing.

I have a process I use with teams called StoryMythos; I have shared it hundreds of times at hundreds of workshops all around the world. Like everything I have talked about so far, no tool will write your story for you or guarantee the story is any good, but tools can help you start to lay things out and see what you are working with. Tools are a way to brainstorm story ideas. They are a way to see if you have a good insight to run with. Then you need to practice, practice, practice (yes, I will continue to repeat that).

For this book, I am sharing an abbreviated version of my StoryMythos process, just three basic steps:

1. First, develop your theme (which we covered in the chapter on sequels)—remember, that is the human truth behind your story. It's the story's deeper meaning. It's what your story is *really* about.
2. Next, develop a story pitch—a simple summation of your story that leaves the audience wanting more. It represents the story you will tell to bring your theme to life.
3. Finally, with a good theme and pitch in hand, write your first story outline using the seven-stage simplified Hero's Journey structure I mentioned earlier.

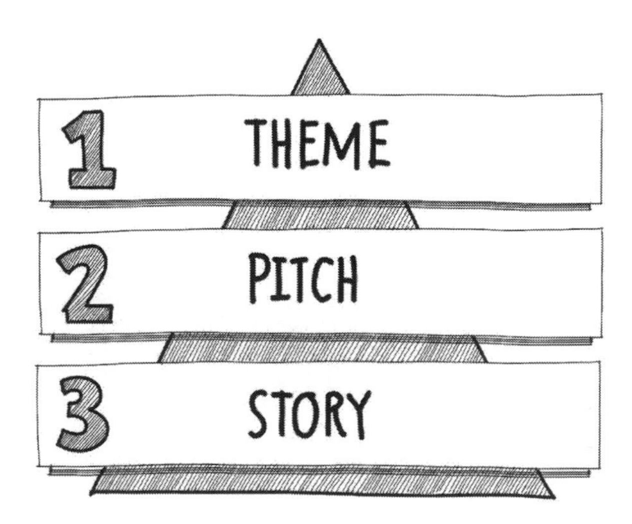

Note that writing the story outline is *last*. That may not seem logical, but I have found it much more constructive to first understand the deeper meaning behind your story and then effectively pitch it. Once you can do those, the larger story can become a lot easier to craft.

> When you learn to synopsize a story, you learn to construct it.[103]
>
> **—Philip Dunne, Hollywood screenwriter**

If you dive headfirst into writing the full story, the danger is that you can get caught up in what is called exposition: too much information, too much background, too much setup, too much description, too many messages, and a simple lack of direction. The story can begin to wander.

If you had just thirty seconds to get someone interested in your story, what would you tell them? The business world calls this the "elevator pitch," which is basically a quick story you tell someone while sharing an elevator. That is a very short time to convince your audience that your idea is worth hearing more about.

Mastering the idea of the pitch is all about being able to explain your story quickly and with power. If the theme is the deeper meaning at the core of your story, then the pitch is the story hook—the summary of the story you would tell to bring that theme to life.

Since we already covered *theme*, let's go deeper into the *pitch* and then the *seven-stage hero's journey!*

CHAPTER FOURTEEN

Leave Your Audience Wanting More

Hollywood receives thousands and thousands of screenplays each year. They can't read them all, so they need a way to help sift through the ideas. That is where the pitch sometimes comes in. Your pitch may play a key role in whether your idea ever gets read or not.

Pitches are usually pretty short and can range from a sentence or two to a page. The way to think about a pitch is not the quantity of words, but the quality. The words you use matter! You must create interest and emotion with your idea, even with a limited time or space.

As an example, let me return to the Hemingway Challenge I mentioned earlier. According to the legend, Hemingway crafted this six-word "novel" (or some variation thereof) on a bet:[104]

For sale, baby shoes. Never worn.

Read that line a few times. Wow! What do you think this story is about? Did you instinctively take this to a sad place by assuming something bad must have happened? Most people do.

What is amazing about this is that I gave no context, setup, or background that would have necessarily led you to that place. Based on only six words, you were able to take the story somewhere and fill in the gaps in a way that produced an emotional response. Whether its attribution to Hemingway is historical or not, the truth remains that good storytellers understand that people look for a way to invest emotionally in a story.

I was an intern at P&G in 1996, and I had come in early one day. As I rounded the corner and got on the elevator, another person was standing there. I instantly recognized this person because I had seen a painting of him in one of the halls. It was our then-CEO, Mr. John Pepper.

John is one of the nicest people you will ever meet and a legend at P&G. He is easy to talk to, loves the company, and loves to hear people's stories. But all I knew as a twenty-two-year-old college intern was that this was the CEO of one of the biggest companies in the world, so of course I was nervous, very nervous. I got on the elevator, looked up briefly, said hello, and quickly turned to face the door.

I remember thinking, "He's going to say something to me, I just know it," so I scrambled to think of something clever to say. Sure enough, as soon as the elevator doors closed, being the very nice and approachable person that he is, he turned toward me, said good morning, and introduced himself.

After we shook hands and I introduced myself, he asked me, *"So Shane, tell me, what are you working on and why is it important to the company?"*

Yikes! A panic set in as I scrambled for an inspiring, clever way to reply.

I ended up giving him the definition of what an industrial designer does. A definition? Is that what he was asking for? That would be like a market researcher saying, "I am a researcher, and my job is to spend time with customers and better understand their needs to develop new product ideas." That doesn't leave me wanting to hear more. That is what every researcher does!

A definition is a functional statement with no emotion and no story, and Mr. Pepper knew what a researcher (and a designer) does. What he was looking for was for me to tell a quick, powerful story about my favorite current project and how it was going to touch and improve our consumers' lives.

Don't make the mistake I did. Have your "CEO elevator pitch" always handy. Even if you don't ever run into your CEO, it is still something you can use and is a great practice. How would you pitch what your job is and what you uniquely do? What would your personal pitch be?

If someone in an elevator asked you what you love about your company, what would you say? Don't give them the quick generic corporate-speak version. Instead, have a quick story to tell, one that leaves them wanting to hear more. Keep in mind this popular adage, often attributed to Albert Einstein: "If you can't explain it simply, then you don't understand it well enough."[105]

Part of an elevator pitch is its brevity. But, the more important part is if it actually catches attention. The way you know that an "elevator pitch" worked is they put their hand over the door to keep it from closing. They want to stay a little longer to ask you more. Maybe they even ask you to walk with them the rest of the way so they can hear more.

The goal is to create such interest that they want to give you more *time*; and remember that time is the most valuable currency in storytelling. If someone is willing to give more to you, you have touched them and their emotions in meaningful way. Well done! Today, if someone asked me what I do, I would say something like, "I help people tell stories, and in my twenty-one years at the largest consumer products company in the world, I have yet to find a business problem that can't be solved with what works in *Star Wars*...and that is simply having a great story." I would hope that statement would get them to ask "so, how do you do that?" and the conversation would go from there.

Key elements every pitch should have

Creating and writing a pitch is not easy. It definitely requires a mastery of language, lots of iteration, and, you guessed it, practice. I would recommend that you go online and research both "story pitches" and another term for them, "loglines." There are a lot of great articles out there on both, and they are valuable resources. When I have teams write pitches in workshops, I make sure they try a few different variations. The simplest way to get started is to write down three of the basics:

1. Who is your hero?
2. What are they are trying to do?
3. What (or who) is in their way?

Now you need to get those elements into a succinct, powerful storyline. Let me share a couple of my favorite examples. The first one is from a great book called *101 Things I Learned in Film School* by Neil Landau.[106]

> A curmudgeonly weatherman keeps waking up on the same day.

That is a pitch for the film *Groundhog Day*—a classic comedy starring Bill Murray. Let's unpack this pitch so you can see all the information squeezed into ten words.

- Who is the protagonist? *The weatherman.*
- Who or what is the antagonist? *Waking up on the same day.*
- What is the setting? *The same day. A twenty-four-hour period starting with a "waking" moment.*
- What is the emotional hook? *Well, let's dig into this one a little.*

Have you ever had déjà vu? How would you describe the emotion you felt? Most people would say "weird" or "surprising." Now, let's say you realize you have been living the same day five times in a row. What emotion would you feel now? Say, "anger," "fear," or maybe "frustration." Now, let's say it is day thirty of you reliving the same day. What would your emotion be? What would anger turn into over thirty days? Most likely "hopelessness," "despair," or even "insanity."

Do you remember how Bill Murray's character eventually tries to stop the cycle he is in? He tries to commit suicide. So, what the emotional hook unpacks to is that, depending on how long you repeat the "same day," it can go from surprise to frustration to hopelessness. A nice range of emotions to play with.

Another key word in this is "weatherman." Why a weatherman and not an accountant or a lawyer or a zookeeper? Because one thing a weatherman loves in particular about his job is that the weather changes every day, and if they are reliving the same day over and over, then the weather isn't changing and their job is pointless, too.

All of this is unpacked from ten words. The writer of this pitch understands language and knows what the most important part of the story is. There are clearly many other characters in the story, there are many different scenes, and many different actions and events. Notice it doesn't even mention the words *Groundhog Day* or the main character's name. Why? Because those don't really add anything to understanding the basic story.

Do you know what the most important part of your story is? Could you take your next presentation and send me a one-sentence pitch for it that would leave me so intrigued that I was excited to spend a full hour with you?

How about this pitch example from IMDB.com:

> A young FBI cadet must confide in an incarcerated and manipulative killer to receive help catching another serial killer.[107]

There are two key words in this one: "young" and "confide." Confiding is not just a casual chat or conversation. Confiding is giving trust and providing personal information. How would you like to be a new hire in an organization and have to exchange personal information and emotions with a serial killer just so you can try to catch another one?

Now, let's put the pitch idea into a business or leadership example from Chip and Dan Heath's book *Made to Stick*. Imagine if this was how JFK's "space race" speech had started:

> Our mission is to become the international leader in the space industry through maximum team-centered innovation and strategically targeted aerospace initiatives...[108]

Just rolls right off the tongue doesn't it? What does this actually say we are trying to do? Lots of buzzwords that don't say much. Too complicated and unclear. A corporate lingo bingo game.

This is what "corporate speak" can sound like if you aren't careful. Fortunately, this wasn't his speech. Instead, his famous speech was something closer to this:

> We will put a man on the moon and return him safely by the end of the decade.

With that statement, do you know what we need to do? Do you know when we need to do it by? Do you know what success looks like? "Yes" to all. We also know that it won't be easy—it will be risky and very dangerous, so there is a lot of emotion built into that.

Less can be more and usually is. I once heard an instructor at a seminar say that if you can't get me excited with fifty words, then making it five thousand probably won't help.

Now, imagine if this was your brand's "vision manifesto":

> We will lead global growth as an iconic brand with consumer-noticeable innovation, holistically designed from purchase to use and deliver superior value to our customers and shareholders.

Helpful? If someone asked what your company does, would this be your elevator pitch? Please no! This is a description of every brand in the world. The words are all true, and every company would want these things, but it doesn't capture one unique thing about the company or its people. All of these things are a standard issue to succeed in any business...in any industry.

Let's practice creating pitches

I conduct story workshops at many different elementary and junior high schools in Cincinnati, and, a year ago, I did a pitch exercise with a seventh and eighth grade advanced placement English class. I came in for a few hours, did some exercises with the students, and at the end asked them to write a pitch for their favorite Disney film. They did an awesome job! One of my favorites is from an eighth grader who wrote this:

Hamlet *with animals*

Do you know what Disney film that is? First you have to know what *Hamlet* is really about, and she did. Bravo! She also understood that *Hamlet* is about family betrayal, brother betraying brother. Have you guessed what the film is yet? *Lion King* is *Hamlet* with animals. That pitch showed me that she really understood the simplest way to express the story. That is a great pitch!

"What if…?" statements

Another kind of pitch worth taking a look at is called the "What if" statement. I find these very helpful to use for product, service, and brand stories. They are simply a provocative question that leaves you thinking about the answer.

Here is a movie example. What if you could go to the zoo today and see real dinosaurs? That is a "What if" pitch idea for a movie called *Jurassic Park*.

Here is one that is more product-centric and was said by a very well-known innovator named Steve Jobs not long ago: *What if you could have 1,000 songs in your pocket?* What product is that? Of course, it is the iPod.[109]

This question threw everything people knew about portable music right out the window, and everyone wanted to understand *how*. The iPod changed music forever.

What if you leveraged crowdsourcing for solving big company problems? Maybe you have heard of the XPrize. What becomes possible when you open up a problem for everyone around the world to work on together, regardless of the company they are currently with? When a company focuses on a problem, they are limited by the resources they have available. However, if you open the problem up to the public and make a nice prize as an incentive—it is amazing what people from around the world can solve.

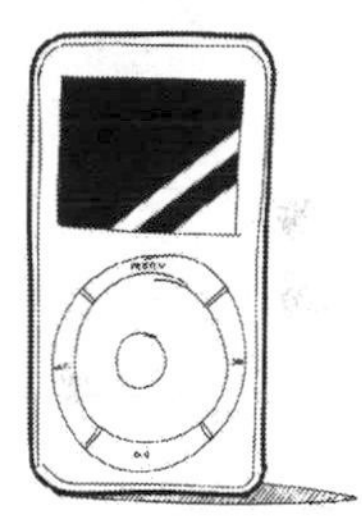

Here are few more "What ifs" to consider:

- What if your phone could find and pay for a ride to anywhere? (Uber)
- What if you could enjoy the comforts of a home anywhere you traveled? (Airbnb)
- What if you had a personal navigator to anywhere in the world right on your phone? (Google Maps)
- What if laundry soap was something you could throw in versus pour? (Tide PODS)

Practice "What if…" pitches with your team for a current or upcoming project. They are a clever way to help you test how interesting your idea really is. It can also help you decide or reconsider what the most interesting part of the project may be. Use a "What if…" for the title of an email! It may make the difference between someone reading it and deleting it.

I recommend that you do theme and pitch exercises in fast, five-minute iterations and then share. Get reactions, do some voting, and move to another round with the lead directions. Fast turnaround. Diverge and converge. If you spend too much time on a single iteration, you wordsmith yourself to death. You can always do detailed copywriting later once you start to get some lead directions.

Linking your theme and pitch

Now that you understand and have a theme and pitch, you need to make sure they relate to each other.

Although they're two separate parts of the story process, they both must build on each other. They are cumulative. Again, the theme is what your story is really about (remember, usually brought to life by a great quote or parable), and the pitch is an inspiring summary of the story.

So, a pitch for *Jurassic Park* may be "What if you

could go to the zoo today and see real dinosaurs?" The theme for *Jurassic Park* could be "Just because science can doesn't mean science should." Do you see how the two relate to each other? One adds more to the other. One is more of a story and the other is more of the lesson. The theme may be up at 10,000 feet and then the pitch gets close to ground level.

The theme also helps make clear what direction the pitch (and ultimately the story) is going in. If I only gave you the "What if," then the *Jurassic Park* example could go either way—it may turn out good, or it may turn out bad. Put that theme in, the moral to the story, and you now know it's not going to end well.

One of the fun exercises I do at new hire events is to have each attendee prepare a personal pitch centered around an "I'll bet you didn't know this about me" kind of story. I then ask them to decide what the theme is for their story.

Here are a couple of my favorite examples that demonstrate how they are linked and how they each build on each other. Note: I always have them read the pitch first and then end with the theme.

> PITCH: An established professional couple in the big city thinks a child would be an easy addition to their lives—then they have twins.
>
> THEME: Nothing changes you like being a parent.

Do you see the relationship? Even though you

may not know all the story details yet, you can see how the theme could come to life within that storyline. Here is another one.

> PITCH: An English teacher in a strange country finds friendship in a neighborhood child who does not speak.
>
> THEME: No matter how different we all are, we can always relate to each other in some way.

Of course, the objective for this exercise is to avoid the usual "intro" statements that many people give like "school, degree, favorite hobbies, and nickname." What is great about having a clear theme is that it can help you edit and make sure you only talk the parts that fit that story.

A warning for brands as you create a pitch: They are *not* sell lines or taglines. Most brands have a tagline. Things like "Just do it" (Nike), "Strong enough for a man, but made for a woman" (Secret), and "Drivers wanted" (VW)—those are great tag/sell lines but aren't quite a story. Unless you know the brand top to bottom, those don't actually say much and could apply to a lot of things.

I mentioned this earlier, but if the line you create would look good on a package or print advertisement, then it is probably *not* a pitch.

So, the tagline for *Jaws* was "You'll never go in the water again."[110] That isn't really a story, but with the visual on the movie poster of a shark coming up under a swimmer, you get it. The pitch would be something closer to "An island police chief must battle a gigantic man-eating shark because of a greedy town council that wants the beaches to stay open."

Here is the tagline from one of my other favorite movies: "*In space no one can hear you scream.*" That was the tagline for a movie called *Alien.*[111] Another classic tagline by the way, but doesn't really tell you much about the story…other than it may be scary and that sound doesn't travel in space.

The pitch for *Alien* could have been something like "*Jaws* in Space." There is a legend, by the way, that this was the actual pitch. Not sure if that is true, but a cool statement nonetheless. Both movies have very similar overall story structures. Both have a ship, both have a crew, and in both the crew is picked off one by one. Both end with the hero fighting the beast mano a mano. Both end with the hero using part of their environment to kill the beast—an air tank with *Jaws* and an airlock in *Alien.* Both put people below the top of the food chain, and both deal with scary places where you can't see well—like the darkness of space or under the surface of the water.

A pitch helps share the story while a tagline only works after you have a clear story and give people time to learn and study it. Taglines also usually require visuals.

Once you have decided on your theme and you have created a pitch, it is time to start writing the actual story.

WORKBOOK

Chapter Fourteen Questions

Question: Take one of your favorite movies and create a pitch for it. Share your pitch and see what people think. Did you capture the essence of the film in an intriguing way?

Question: Create a pitch for one of your current brand projects. Share it. Does it make people curious or interested to hear more?

Chapter Fourteen Notes

CHAPTER FIFTEEN

Time to Write Your Story

> If you are going to have a story, have a big story or none at all.[112]
>
> —**Joseph Campbell**

The simplistic Hero–Obstacle–Treasure structure we discussed earlier will help you look at the "broad strokes" of your story, but eventually you will need to take it to the next level. For that, you need to return to Joseph Campbell and Christopher Vogler. The Hero's Journey model that was originally proposed by Campbell and then expanded on by Vogler is a wonderful tool to help with story writing (look that up online).

I have read all of Joseph Campbell's writings and cherish Christopher Vogler's book *The Writer's Journey* (third edition).[113] I had the honor of meeting and hosting Christopher Vogler at P&G for a brainstorming event. Both have been huge influences on me and helped me see the movie-to-brand connection. Campbell and Vogler share a lot of understanding and thinking when it comes to the Hero's Journey, and they both have their variations on it.

For example, Campbell had seventeen stages in his Hero's Journey model whereas Vogler reduced that down to twelve. I have my own slight variation when developing a brand story that uses just seven. But, the full versions work too. Use what works best for you. Bottom line, study and learn the Hero's Journey.

Regardless of which you use, what is most important is that you learn and understand what each stage in the journey means, the values each represents, and the role each plays in a story.

Remember, your story needs to be based on emotional understanding and deep human insight; again, there is no formula for that. These stages are not just a code to plug things in, they are a thinking model or even a planning tool. Like everything else we have talked about, it will take … you guessed it, practice and experimentation!

The seven-stage hero's journey

The hero's journey will end up being about two simple things: choice and change. It will involve the choices the hero makes and the change(s) those choices bring about.

I have included a simple visual below of the seven

stages I use. Let's talk about each stage briefly.[114]

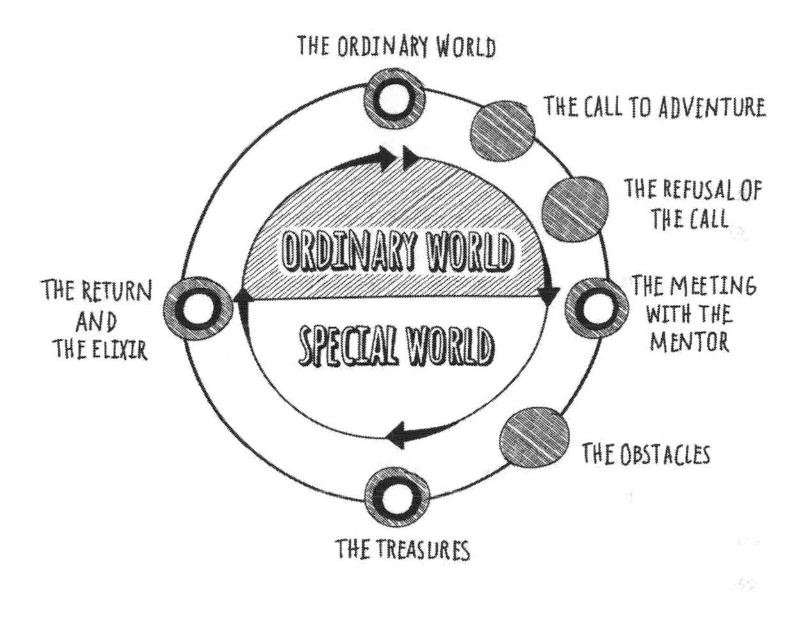

1. The Ordinary World—the setup and challenge

This is about background and the setup needed—what does the audience need to know in the beginning to follow and understand the story? What is needed to "set the stage"? Also, what is out of balance in the hero's life? If nothing is out of balance for the hero, there would be no need for a story. What do they want? What is the simplest way to introduce whom your brand is for and how it can help them?

2. The Call to Adventure—an inciting incident

What is the inciting incident that triggers the hero's consideration to change or try something different? What catalyst presents itself, forcing a consideration and eventually a decision? In many cases, this "call" is brought to the hero by a character called "the herald"—a message bringer. The herald could be anything from an event, to social media, to TV ads, to word of mouth. Something must happen or be shared in order to make our hero consider a change.

3. The Refusal to Accept the Call—doubts and disbelief

Being a hero is tough work. The refusal of the call to adventure involves dealing with the doubts and disbeliefs that a hero has about the journey or the perils of change. Remember, change is scary. Change means risk, and risk means the potential for failure. Anytime you think of trying something different or making a change, there is usually a little voice in your head that will remind you to "be careful." This voice is your internal "devil's advocate." It could be a quick thought, but there is always a need to be cautious and make sure you're not jumping into something you shouldn't. Sometimes even the most exciting call to adventure is still refused by the hero simply because of fear or uncertainty. Just because you advertise doesn't mean anyone will be interested or care.

Try to predict what the refusals may be for your hero, and then you can prepare for them. To do this, of course, you have to know your hero very well. This is also where the importance of the motivation or treasure comes in. No one wants to deal with the troubles of change if the reward is weak. Think about why you turn down many calls to adventure...it is probably because the reward doesn't outweigh the risks.

4. The Meeting with the Mentor—guidance and help items

This is where the company, brand, or product comes into the story. How will the consumer get past their refusals and ultimately deal with the obstacles in the way of the treasure?

A mentor has to step in and provide two pieces of help—guidance and something practical to help with the obstacles. Remember, that doesn't have to be something physical; it can be knowledge, a method, a service, or just an insight. Good mentors are authentic and feel "real." As we discussed earlier, a mentor doesn't have to be a person. It is anything that guides and inspires.

The mentor helps create a line in the sand for the

hero that, when crossed, will signal that the adventure is in progress. They help move the hero forward and embrace a change.

5. The Obstacles—the key challenges to be faced

The hero has decided to go on the journey and then enters what Campbell would call the "special world." This new world should look and feel very different to what we saw in the "ordinary world." With that new world there will be both known and unknown challenges. What key obstacles must be dealt with? How will your hero truly be tested? The obstacles represent both small and large tests that your hero must find a way through. They basically help the hero learn and use new skills. Failure could be part of this stage. After all, that is one of the best ways to learn. So, if your consumer decides to try your new product, change their current process, take a leap of faith, what changes and risks will they have to be ready for?

In some cases, the obstacles follow a linear path and raise the emotional stakes with each passing stage (big to bigger to biggest). This is where you want to use the climax diagram we used earlier—the Emotion against Time chart. The further the story goes, the more emotion you must engage from your hero and your audience. That is why the climax is never in the middle act and instead is always at the end. This is also why you don't want the most powerful part of your presentation to be in the first act.

Obstacles are critical because they help the audience develop and feel empathy for the hero. In mythology, the hero usually dies here (literally or in many cases figuratively) and is reborn, changed.

In product terms, this would be the same. Hopefully, after your consumer uses your product, begins to learn it, and sees what it can do and how it helps, they can no longer go back to the way things were before. The transformation becomes significant.

6. The Treasure(s)—short-term reward

What rewards will the hero find along the way? These are the "changes in moment" for the hero. They can be relatively small in the grand scheme of things and really are there to give the hero a boost of confidence to keep going. Being a hero is tough, after all.

There are usually a series of treasures scattered across the different journey stages. These rewards are pats on the back, saying "good job" and "keep up the good work." These are usually quick to find and very recognizable. This could be the result you see from using a new product for that first time. Or maybe a surprising benefit from a new service that you didn't know was there. The bigger insight or moral to the story may not be evident yet, but these treasures keep the hero's energy up.

7. The Return and Recognizing the Elixir—long-term meaning

What is the return? The return is a stage that heroes must go through after they get past the big obstacle, the one that really needs dealing with. It is seeing and recognizing the "ripples in the pond" that occur from the journey, regardless if it ends in success or failure. What will change now? What will happen next? What does the hero's "new world" look like? What new obstacles may be created because of their "triumph"? What will change or be learned if the journey ends with a failure?

You must make this understanding clear and inevitable. To do this, you need to clearly articulate what was learned and how it will affect the hero's world long-term. As they deal with the return, they also must realize what the true "elixir" is.

What is an elixir? If a treasure is a "change in moment," then the elixir is a "change in life." They are large, epiphany-like moments where a new bar has been set, where a new way of thinking or approaching a problem happens, or where life changes in some way. It is the deeper meaning and where your theme really becomes clear.

Elixirs can take a lot of time to realize, like when you look back on a particular project years later and remember how tough it was at the time, but that you learned a very important lesson from it that you still use today.

You may not actually see or understand the elixir for months, or even years, since it usually takes time and many life experiences to see the bigger picture.

An elixir is very powerful, though, and can forever alter how a hero will approach life from that moment forward. Campbell called it the ultimate boon that is shared with everyone and eventually creates a new ordinary world. Vogler said it is the proof that the hero has been there and learned something. If the hero doesn't come back from a great journey with something to show for it, "the hero, or someone else, is doomed to repeat the ordeals until the lesson is learned."[115] Sounds like a company, doesn't it?

Practice these and you will start to see them everywhere. Take these seven stages, watch any TV show or movie this weekend, and try and pull them out. Look at one of your favorite personal stories and break it down using them. Pull up one of your favorite presentations and see if they are there. Look at them with a broad set of eyes, don't get too caught up in the order, simply recognize the key meaning and details behind each stage.

The seven-sentence brand story exercise

Once you understand the stages, I have a quick exercise you can use to get your team writing. I call it the *Seven-Sentence Exercise.*

Start by deciding who your "audience" is for the story you want to create (e.g., is it your target consumer, management, shareholders, a retailer, etc.). Next, have the team write a story about your product or brand using only one sentence for each of the Hero's Journey stages. Just one sentence, no more. So, that would be a total of seven. This will force them to really think about and write down the most important sentence to represent each stage. This will also allow them to see if they truly understand the values behind each and how those could affect the larger story.

Like the previous exercises I have shared, have your team do this quickly with a couple of refinement stages. Give them twenty minutes maximum to do this exercise.

After the first draft is completed, get some feedback (focusing on the audience chosen). Have a few fresh eyes and ears come in and hear the story as well (friends who can play devil's advocate). Take that feedback, tweak the story, and share it again.

It is okay if the story is a bit "choppy" at this stage. I mean, there are only seven sentences, don't get too hung up on wordsmithing just yet. Just get the idea down on paper.

Once you get a strong overall direction going, you can start to add more sentences to each of the stages. You can start to create bridges between each of the stages. Start small and work your way to making the story bigger and better. It can sometimes be much easier to add than to cut away, and be sure to only add what is needed. I have found that doing it this way helps slowly add meat to the "story bones," and you have your theme and pitch to keep the content honest and focused. It should all tie together.

For fun, let's dissect a movie and a product using the Seven-Sentence Story method. I can take any movie, regardless of length, and create a single sentence for each of these steps in the film. The steps aren't always in linear order; they can be moved around, repeated, etc., but they are usually always there in one way or another.

If you can't take your product or brand and create a seven-sentence story for it, then you may not really know what the actual story is yet. As stated earlier, you have to choose a hero (your *who*) before you write the story. Who is the story for? For example, will your story be about the consumer's journey, an employee's journey, or the company's journey? Those will all look a bit different.

Let's do this exercise for *Star Wars Episode IV: A New Hope*. Remember, try and use only one sentence for each of the stages.

1. The Ordinary World—An evil empire is ruling the land, a rebellion fights against them, and a young farmer is bored with his life and longs to be part of the adventure.
2. Call to Adventure—Two helpers show up at the farm and, while working with them, our hero stumbles upon a secret message about a princess captured by the empire—our hero becomes curious and excited to help.
3. The Refusal of the Call—Our hero wants to rescue the princess but feels trapped as he has work to do on the farm, so he decides he really can't do anything to help.
4. The Meeting with the Mentor—A wise local hermit inspires and guides our hero by introducing him to a powerful ancient religion called the Force and by giving him his dead father's sword.
5. The Obstacles—After his family is killed, the young farmer decides to join the hermit to rescue the princess from the empire's stronghold, which is a long, perilous journey far away.
6. The Treasures—After several harrowing battles, he rescues the princess and escapes the stronghold with a secret that can destroy the empire's base.
7. The Return and the Elixir—After accidently leading the empire to the hidden rebel base, a huge battle erupts and the farmer-turned-

> rebel hero uses the Force to destroy the empire's stronghold, quickly realizing that he has taken his first step into a whole new world.

There you go. The two-hour film summarized in essentially seven sentences. Are there a lot of details missing? Absolutely, tons, but that is not the point of doing this. The point is to show that you know what the most important part of each stage is, the values that the hero deals with, the key transformation steps that occur, and perhaps the deeper meaning behind each stage. Simple and quick.

Star Wars is about following your dreams, working together, and having hope. Luke wanted adventure but he just needed a little push to take that first hard step—as many of us do.

Did you notice that when you boil the core story down (and remove the sci-fi references), it starts to look and feel like a classic "knight in shining armor" fairy-tale? *Star Wars* is a story filled with references to many mythologies. Campbell was one of George Lucas's mentors for the film, and it is a mix of mythological elements, from the lone western gunslinger to knights in shining armor to the skill and discipline of the samurai.

The Hero's Journey construct has such breadth that it can be used across an almost infinite set of problems and planning needs.

I have seen school teachers use it for lesson planning, physical trainers use it for health goals, and there are books like *Resonate* by Nancy Duarte that use it as a presentation planning tool (a great book, by the way, pick it up). It is a structure that has always been there and is ready for you to try.

Let's do another quick practice, but instead of a movie, let's use a brand and product. This time I will share the seven sentences but instead show what it looks like once I have added more details and additional content. The hero for this story is the consumer—the consumer being me—and the product being a vacuum cleaner.

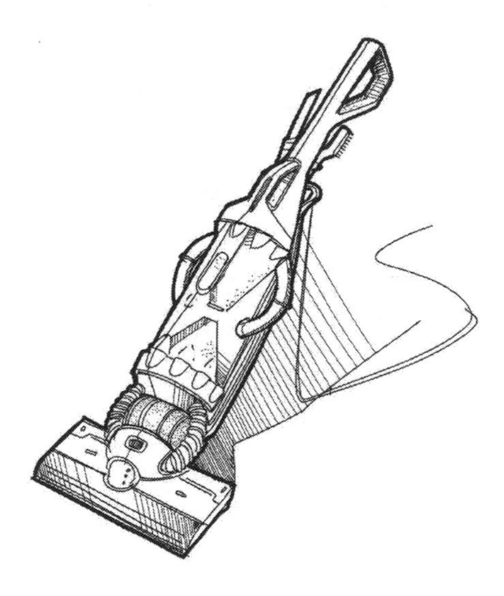

I am a loyal Dyson vacuum user. In my opinion, it is the best vacuum you can buy. My wife and I are very loyal to that brand. So, what was the *Ordinary World*? Do you remember what that category was like before Dyson? Vacuum cleaners used bags that were in zippered pouches attached to the back of the handle. You couldn't really see any of the dirt you ever picked up because the bags were opaque. You also had to keep a supply of bags in your house. But hey, it all seemed to work fine. I would run my vacuum over dirt on the floor and it would be gone. Problem solved…or was there a better way?

But then a *Call to Adventure* happened: I started to see ads and read articles about how regular vacuums lose suction over time, and that their performance degrades.

Honestly, my first reaction was to *Refuse the Call* because it sounded like marketing fluff to me. Like I said, I could see that my current vacuum picked up dirt. What were they talking about?

But then a *Mentor* appeared when I saw this British engineer named James Dyson. James talked about how he liked to fix the simple things in life, things that could be better and easier—household items that were taken for granted. He then explained that he set out to redesign the vacuum cleaner and demonstrated how the performance dropped over time and how his new "Cyclone" technology prevented that.

As an industrial designer, when he showed the actual Dyson vacuum at the end of the ad, I honestly was blown away. I had never seen a vacuum that looked like that. It looked like something from the future or a prop in a sci-fi film. It also showed up in several design magazines.

It was a bold statement in the world of mundane vacuum cleaners. I had to get a closer look and dropped by a store to see one the next time I was out shopping.

When I saw it in person for the first time, it was

incredible. I marveled at its merging of form and function. But I was also instantly hit by one of the largest *Obstacles* of the story—the price! Wow, this vacuum was almost four times what my current one had cost!

However, believing in the mentor and the story the brand had told me so far, I made it past that obstacle. I purchased one and took it home, excited to give it a try. The *Treasures* were instant (remember that treasures are the "changes in moment," quick boosts of confidence for the hero). It sounded more powerful. It glided across the carpet. And wow, emptying a Dyson was so easy and so much cleaner than emptying and replacing the traditional bags.

One of the biggest treasures was so simple and a game-changer for the entire category. Dyson showed you all the dirt you had picked up! The collection chamber for a Dyson was clear. What a great way to feel like you had really done something! You could actually see the amount of filth that had been removed from the floors. Brilliant.

Finally, the *Elixir*: As the years passed, we bought a Dyson cordless vacuum cleaner for our kitchen, and we realized that we could never go back to vacuums with bags. The transformation was clear, and we couldn't go back to the old way.

Dyson had not only set a new bar for me in vacuums, but for other categories too. I mean, if this kind of innovation could be done for a vacuum, why couldn't it be done for some of the other seemingly unchanging household products sitting in my cupboards and on my counters?

Great stories always bring change

Great products can change society by inspiring the story to change. They can ask the ever-important story questions: "So, why can't we...?" or "I wonder what would happen if...?" That was the same question, you may remember, I asked as a kid when I would watch my favorite movies.

It all comes back to the power of story.

Remember earlier when we talked about transformation? Dyson is a great example of having a clear before and after. If great products are taken away from the hero in the "after," they will miss them and quickly realize that they don't want to go back to a time without them. That means they have power, a lot of power.

On the other hand, if a consumer can give up your product and feel no emotion or loss, then how powerful could your story actually be? In short, you don't have one.

You can also use the Hero's Journey to help plan in-store displays, events, or immersive consumer experiences (to see an example of how I have used it at P&G, just Google "P&G Lofts").

Let me show you an example of how you can take the same basic technology and bring it to life in very different ways. Let's use a water ride at a theme park. One example I will show uses a story and the Hero's Journey, and the other really focuses just on the technology itself. Neither is right or wrong...they are both choices and it depends on what you are trying to do. I think you will see, though, that in the end, one has far more power than the other.

Have you ever been on a water ride at a theme park or amusement park? The log flumes, rapids, whitewater rafts, etc. Most parks have a water ride of some sort. Water rides all have one simple promise and objective—to get you wet! Now, some deliver better than others but they all honestly do pretty well. It is a simple technology that almost every brand of park can deliver.

But let's discuss two very different versions of how that technology can be brought to life.

I live near an amusement park. It's local and known throughout the area. It's a very fun place to spend a Saturday, there are lots of great thrill rides and we normally get season passes for our kids each year. One ride there is called Congo Falls. It is a water ride where you get into a boat, float along a river, and then plummet down a slide and get soaking wet. It works, and you definitely scream on the way down.

Close your eyes and say "Congo Falls" in your head; what do you see? What sounds do you hear, what do you smell, and what does the environment look like? Tell me the story that the name brings.

Whenever I ask this question, almost everyone provides the same general answers. In their mind they see palm trees, vines, beautiful flowers, rushing rapids, dangerous rocks, and the sounds of monkeys, exotic birds, and distant native drums. There are maybe crocodiles in the water as you float along. Also, ride operators with safari-type clothes and hats, and a queue through humid jungle terrain with a mysterious mist and lush overgrown cover. Perhaps even old expedition crates lying around and fun jungle-themed merchandise being sold at the gift shop (shirts like "I survived the expedition to Congo Falls").

I am sure you thought of many of those ideas, too. But, you actually don't see or experience *any* of those things on this ride. It has a rich name with no real story behind the execution. You essentially walk through a standard aluminum bar queue, get into a standard boat, go up a mechanical hill, and then immediately shoot down it. No real gift shop experience. No use of sound effects, themed media, or scent. The operators aren't in character.

Now, it is a ride that completely delivers on its functional promise—you get soaked. The technology works great. But it could also be the water ride at any other park anywhere. If you wanted, you could bring it to life very differently through a rich backstory. Of course, that would require more budget, time, planning, etc. So, it all comes down to what you really want to do with your brand or product experience. Congo Falls is not a journey and it doesn't really have a story (other than to get wet), and that may be totally fine for what that brand wanted. But never underestimate the power a story can bring to even the simplest technology.

At Walt Disney World, there is also a water ride. It is called Splash Mountain. It is located in Frontierland, which is all about historic Americana—the themes of exploration, discovery, American Revolutionary history, the Deep South, and the Wild West.

That was a time filled with exciting events like the gold rush, stagecoaches and cowboys, trains connecting new territories, and massive riverboats churning up and down the Mississippi. It also had powerful characters ranging from our Founding Fathers to Pecos Bill and Tom Sawyer.

Disney ensures that every detail in each land fits the theme. The food, the landscape, the plant life, the music, the decor, the employee costumes—everything.

For the water ride in Frontierland, they looked to a classic southern Americana folklore character called Br'er Rabbit. Br'er Rabbit was featured in the 1946 Disney film *Songs of the South.*

In that story, Br'er Rabbit uses his wits (instead of brawn) to escape his enemies. He fights authority figures and likes to bend social conventions. However, he is constantly being hunted by his two archnemeses, Br'er Fox and Br'er Bear, who want to catch and eat him.

As you walk up to the ride, you are greeted by an amazing vista over Br'er Rabbit's world, called Chick-A-Pin Hill. As soon as you walk through the gate, the story begins.

While you wait in line, you get to meet the characters, hear the classic southern banjo and fiddle music, and see the world our hero lives in. You even get to go into his rabbit hole, meet some of his friends, and see pictures of his favorite places hanging on his wall. You travel along with him right through the story. You then find yourself in a logging town where you board your transport.

From there, you start the ride and make your way through several story scenes based on the Walt Disney version of the folktale. All of this follows the Hero's Journey framework.

It is a progressing storyline starting with the rabbit leaving home to find some adventure, and he quickly finds trouble instead. Before he leaves, he receives some advice from his mentor—a talking bluebird (you know, "...on your shoulder")—to be careful of the Fox and Bear, but he ignores the counsel and is soon captured by his enemies.

When they are preparing to cook him—it is during the time you are climbing up the final climactic hill (you know, the "click-click-click" part as you slowly ascend and get ready for the drop)—the rabbit convinces his enemies, using trickery (reverse psychology), that being put into the briar patch at the bottom of the hill would be a fate far worse than death.

The Fox and Bear hate him so much that they would rather torture him than eat him, so they throw him off the top of the hill (and you go with him) where he lands safely in the briar patch (you do too, and get soaked on the way down).

But the ride is not over. We still need to see the Elixir, which is a final scene showing him back in front of his house telling the bluebird that he has learned his lesson and that he will be more careful next time. I love it!

Using a well-crafted story as a way to immerse the guests in each ride is the Disney way. Disney does not necessarily expect each person to recognize the stages I outlined above, but people remember this ride because it has a great story. It has its own story as much as it is part of the larger Disney park story.

Also, think about how much easier it would be to create a ride with a story backdrop like that, how much easier it would be to make decisions on execution details, colors, logos, environments, music, and merchandise.

Disney wants you to always be in a story at the park, and to do that they use the story to guide all their decisions and executions. A ride's core story helps answer many of the executional questions and therefore helps save a lot of time and discussion on why a detail is the right thing to do, even if it potentially costs more. It sets their rides apart from parks that just deliver the basic promise and focus primarily on the technology.

Now, I really enjoy the local amusement park, but I also don't look at it the same way I do Disney World (and neither do my kids). Each is a choice, and the key difference between them is the use (or lack) of a story. The Congo Falls execution could show up in any park in the world, but Splash Mountain is unmistakably Disney.

I recently watched a November 2016 video of Airbnb CEO Brian Chesky introducing their new "Trips" service. Trips is a service that allows customers to book local tours and experiences in the same area in which they book a house, essentially immersing them in the local culture.

In his talk, Brian explains that the inspiration for "Trips" was Joseph Campbell's Hero's Journey. They realized that travel is a lot like what characters experience in great stories. Here is what he said:

> A character starts in their ordinary world. They cross

> the threshold—think *Wizard of Oz*—to this new magical world, where they meet people...they have a moment of transformation and they return to the ordinary world. As the Airbnb team explored the hero's journey, a light bulb went off: sharing homes and rooms is only one small part of a great travel journey. People remember the magic of an experience.[116]
>
> **—Brian Chesky**

Anything that has a great story has the potential to be more memorable, more powerful, and more meaningful. It works in life, so it works for brands and experiences, too.

WORKBOOK

Chapter Fifteen Questions

Question: Using the Seven-Sentence Story exercise, write out the story for your company or brand. What surprises you? Where is the story strong, and where does it need work? Does it sound exciting or flat? Unique or predictable? What needs to be fixed?

____

____

____

____

____

____

____

____

Question: How is your brand an experience? What story could help guide the experience planning and execution?

Chapter Fifteen Notes

CHAPTER SIXTEEN

A Genre for Your Brand

As you create your story, it is helpful to think about genre. Every story has one, and if you don't plan for one, your audience usually will. Intuitively, we look for certain story conventions and expressions in order to decide if a story is a comedy, horror, sci-fi, drama, etc.

Genre is one way that we compartmentalize stories. Genres set the viewer up for what to expect and help the writer set up certain rules of the road.

If you go to a horror movie, both your head and your heart will prepare themselves by expecting some of these rules. For example, you always expect the victims to go and investigate a mysterious noise alone and say, "I'll be right back." You know that probably won't turn out well.

From the execution, you also know that music plays a key role in a scary film, setting a suspenseful mood, like the simple but instantly recognizable score from *Jaws*. Dark visuals, mysterious environments, primal emotions. You get the idea.

Genre for brands works the same. For example, sports brands have a certain set of conventions that you look for in how they talk and express themselves, a certain kind of packaging, symbols, color palettes, etc.

I said "rules," but be careful. Rules can be bent or even broken if needed. So, start with understanding the current rules first before you decide how you want to change them.

Method is a great brand of cleaning products that are unique-looking in the aisle. There was a certain set of "genre" conventions that the appearance of most cleaning products followed. Method decided to break those rules by having a well-known designer, Karem Rashid, design a packaging language that would set them apart.[117]

Method has always tried to push the limits of those category expectations and has done a great job at being distinctive across their several product lines. I am sure that is one of the reasons Target likes them so much—Method appreciates great design just as Target does.

The seven core genres

There are literally hundreds of different genres. But as I dug through them all, read their definitions, and looked at each through more of a brand lens, I found what I believe are the seven core genres of products and brands. I can't find a product that doesn't fit into one of these seven or a combination

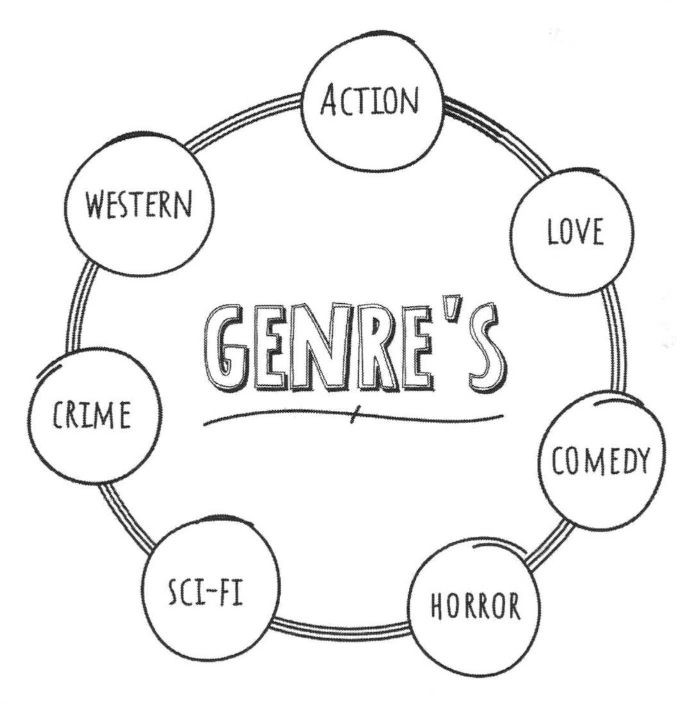

of them.

Combination? What do I mean? Just like in film, it is possible to have what is called a "dual genre," like a "rom-com" (short for romantic comedy). I would not recommend having more than two, though, because it can become a little confusing and disjointed. As you look at the seven below, pay less attention to the titles and focus more on the definitions.

1. Action-Adventure:

A clash of physical forces, sometimes in a different world or other unusual environment. Think exercise brands, bikes and cars, camping, and travel (e.g. Nike, Columbia Sportswear, The North Face, Airbnb).

2. Romance:

To find or keep the love and/or relationship with another. Think brands focused on relationships, whether family, friends, or lovers (e.g. Walt Disney World, Tiffany, Victoria's Secret, and Carnival Cruise Line).

3. Horror-Thriller:

A hero escaping from or defeating a "monster." The monster is anything that the hero is battling, which could be represented by an environment, emotional state, illness, situation, or life stage (e.g. brands like Mucinex, Crest, Farmers Insurance, Tide, LifeLock).

4. Sci-Fi/Fantasy:

Technology and/or magic of an imaginable world. It

focuses on a surprising technology, benefit, or process that creates a "wow" (e.g. Mr. Clean Magic Eraser, iPhone, Google, and Tesla).

5. Crime-Detective:

To expose or find the truth, helping the audience pick a side. Anything that shows a comparison or demo of results, a side-by-side visual, or provides data and facts is a crime-detective (e.g. Surface Pro versus Mac, DiGiorno's versus delivery, Verizon versus AT&T, Febreze actually removing the bad scent versus a regular spray simply covering it up).

6. Western:

A lone hero fighting existing systems or norms while gaining supporters and creating a movement or change. This is where the "Constructive Deviant" can come in. Any brand that takes a rebel-like stand or attitude and wants to shift or change the status quo (e.g. Apple, Harley Davidson, Method, and Southwest).

7. Comedy:

Laughter and hilarious results. Any brand that uses humor or sarcasm to build and reinforce their character and story (e.g. Old Spice, Allstate Mayhem, Charmin, and Dollar Shave Club).

So, pick a brand and ask yourself, "which one is it?" Most are pretty clear. Is it a sci-fi or a horror?

Or maybe it is two, like a western-comedy (like Dollar Shave Club could be).

Once you understand what it is, ask yourself how the conventions of the genre are being leveraged in the various brand expressions. How does it influence the visuals, the sound, the characters? Where are they following the conventions rigidly, and where are they bending or breaking the rules? How are they leveraging the genre's conventions uniquely and making them ownable by the brand?

Harness the power of genres

Knowing the genre always helps design choices and key assets like music, photography style, color choices, etc. Think about the musical differences between a horror and a comedy.

Would slow, gentle music make sense for a Nike running ad? Nope. That is an action story, and action films have fast-paced, high-energy riffs! For Nike, I would also expect to see rapid image changes and dramatic camera angles.

For a Tiffany print ad, I would expect a romantic picture with perhaps high contrast photography with splashes of selective color (like a black and white photo with Tiffany Blue for the box), elegant visuals, classy typeface, soft music (probably piano), and maybe even a couple in a luxurious, intimate situation.

As you are creating your brand story, change the

genre, select a different one, and then ask yourself how your story would need to shift. How about the execution? This is a trick often used by screenwriters when they hit a writing block. It can help you see things from a different angle and trigger serendipitous connections.

Let's say you are working on a comedy but get stuck. Try turning it into a horror story and see what happens. What would need to change? How would the execution need to be adjusted? It doesn't take long to do this exercise, and you may find it not only helps you out of a block, but it may even evolve your story into a more powerful one.

WORKBOOK

Chapter Sixteen Questions

Question: What genre(s) is your current brand story? What other genre(s) could your brand consider and why?

Question: Using your earlier Seven-Sentence Story, share it and ask people what genre they think fits that best. What did they choose and why? Is that the genre you were planning on? If not, what would need to change to make it work?

Chapter Sixteen Notes

CHAPTER SEVENTEEN

A Look Back at the Process and a Few Watch-Outs

Well, there you go: Story 101—and some 201! We've talked over story principles and fundamentals, and we've played around with a few story tools. Although I believe creating a story is an organic process and is very flexible, I usually do follow a particular order in my workshops—let me share it (but bend and break it as needed):

1. With the five story ingredients we discussed in mind, plot out a few of your possible brand or product storylines using the **Hero–Obstacle–Treasure** visual. Try to create three or four directions to start.

2. After you have a few lead directions, develop

a **theme** for each. So, if you have three overall storylines you want to explore, you will need three themes. All three may be different, and that is okay.

3. Then, for each of your different themes you will need a story **pitch**. What story would bring to life your theme and how would you pitch it? Share those with people, get some feedback. Refine as needed. Make sure the pitch and theme fit together in some way. Most importantly, the pitch needs to leave them wanting more! Remember, don't make it five hundred words until you can excite them with fifty.

4. Next, write a **seven-sentence story** for each theme/pitch combo. This will start to unpack the story with more detail and help you decide what the most important parts for each story would be.

5. For each seven-sentence story, decide on the **genre** that would help bring it to life. What genre makes the most sense for each story? Put some visual boards together for each one that start to show the look, tone, and feel. Include elements like font, color palette, photography style, and shape. Pick a soundtrack. Share the execution with people and

get some feedback.

6. Test, refine, and repeat as needed. Remember, never go with a first draft on any of these steps. It is called a first draft for a reason—because it is not supposed to be your last!

7. Finally, select a lead direction and start to add meat to the bones. Write the full story. If needed, create slightly different versions for different heroes to really flush it out. Remember, there is no such thing as one story. It always about who you are telling it to. The brand story you would tell to a customer or retailer may be very different than the version you would tell to an employee. Share and refine again. Repeat and revisit as necessary.

Note: My process changes with each team or group and their objectives. The above is a rough flow that can be shifted and changed as the need arises. I don't believe in "one size fits all."

Bottom line, it's all about iteration, reaction, and refinement. You can put a design thinking approach directly into story development. There should be several diverge/converge steps throughout this process, so do whatever it takes. You can't write *Star Wars* in a day, so don't try.

Remember, it's great that you and your team love your story, but in the business world, you need the audience to love it too. I bet every director loves the movie they launch, but that doesn't mean the audience and critics will. In the end, it will be your audience that matters the most.

Also, getting a great group of individuals together with great insights and great passion does not guarantee a great story. Everyone truly has to be present as part of the team. Let's discuss some of the common pitfalls that you may have to deal with when developing a brand story.

A few watch-outs when creating a story

Developing a story is tough, tedious, and long work. It is not easy, and I always warn the people coming to a workshop that they will leave tired and mentally drained. But, it is also a lot of fun, because creating and telling stories is something we all love doing. My workshops can be half-days to multiple days. Depends on the objectives.

Now, here are some watch-outs to keep in mind as you create your story (and I have mentioned parts of these in earlier chapters as well). They are:

1. The story is not created inside the company or with enough internal involvement.
2. The story avoids detail for the sake of universality or flexibility.
3. The story sounds Pollyanna-ish or avoids reality.

4. The story is created in a day and loses support and momentum quickly.

Any of these can mean the death of a potentially great story. I am sure some of these may sound obvious. The good news is they are all easy problems to fix—you just have to set the proper expectations early on and everyone has to be willing to do the hard work needed.

One of the best places to get a good laugh on some of these problems is Tom Fishburne's comics called *Brand Camp*. His website is www.marketoonist.com. He has some brilliant insight in his cartoons, and several cartoons fit the ideas above. His comics really touch the office humor that we all have seen and been a part of. I mean, why do you think *Dilbert* and a show like *The Office* are so great? Because we know and understand those stories!

It is always ironic how businesses pass around office cartoons, laugh about them, and then proceed to do some of the same things right inside their walls. You can change that!

Let's talk about each watch-out a bit to understand how you may be able to avoid them.

1. The story is not created inside the company.

I personally think way too much creativity is being completely led by outside agencies. I am constantly amazed at the incredible creativity, leadership, and design trainings that companies invest in for their employees to then give creative leadership to teams outside. Create the story inside and then have your outside partners help you finesse it.

There is a big difference between the concepts "partner" and "own." The first is great and can lead to inspired creativity; the second is kind of removed and, I think, lazy. It creates a missed opportunity.

Having outside partners is fantastic, and the best agencies know that and act that way—they bring fresh eyes, an outside perspective, and creative expertise to help solve the problem *with* the internal project team.

At the end of the day, though, the employees must be the owners of all the final executions. After all, it is *their* company and *their* paycheck and *their* legacy. All agencies have other clients and you are but just one.

Have you ever heard this question: "Who are you most passionate about raising? Your kids or someone else's?" As a metaphor for creative work, just remember that people have far more passion for things they helped create and build than ones that are just given to them from the outside to only execute and apply.

So, if an outside agency does *all* of the creative work and then gives it to the marketer inside the company just to execute it, they may not have a ton of passion for it.

Also, never let anyone in the company tell you

that some single person or function owns the story of the brand. Everyone must own the story, everyone plays a role in it, everyone needs to be a part of it, everyone should contribute to it, and, be careful—anyone can also destroy it.

The advertising function (or marketing) *does not* own the story, R&D doesn't own the story, finance doesn't own the story—they are each but one of many functions and disciplines needed for the story to succeed.

If R&D doesn't develop a great technology, then marketing doesn't have much to talk about and advertise; if you don't have a great advertising strategy, then no one may ever know about the technology. If there isn't a good understanding of the business numbers, then both will fail.

The many functions and disciplines in a company are like spokes on a wheel. If one isn't doing its part, the wheel becomes unstable and may even collapse. Always make sure everyone on your team can see their role in the larger story.

Start by removing any functional biases. You don't want each function creating their own story; you just want every person and function to completely understand the larger brand story and then share it through their functional lens.

Whenever I conduct a story workshop, I ask for a multifunctional team, and the first thing I remind everyone is to forget the function and become the brand. I want to use and leverage everyone's insights and creativity to develop the larger narrative. They are all equal partners.

So, first, draft a narrative that *all* functions understand and have a passion for. Then, ask each function to write down what the larger narrative means to their specific discipline.

In a situation where a story is done outside and just given to a team to deliver, the only lens they can apply to it is their functional lens. That means it is not "their kid" and they may have less passion in helping raise it. Agency partners are great, but please do it all together!

2. The story avoids detail for the sake of universality.

A very common mistake in business is to create messages that are too broad or use buzzwords that sound too much like clichéd corporate speak. This problem of "Business Bingo" is very common in mission statements and brand manifestos.

Macro words are the enemy of a great story. You need details! The more macro words you use, the more you're asking your audience to interpret what you actually mean, which forces them to apply subjective interpretation: *What do I think that means?* Do you see a potential problem happening here?

Think in screenplay terms for a second. Of course, scenes change, new content is added, reshoots are done, and improv occurs on set. But a screenplay is the detailed roadmap where it all starts. How helpful would a screenplay be if it used only broad, overarching words with no specific direction? If it had no subtext (clear meaning and action behind the words, deeper meanings, and emotions)? If it used terms like "forward-thinking," "team-focused," and "innovative"?

All we would hear is "Blah, blah, blah." I love Tom Fishburne's cartoon called "Mission Statement," which represents mission statement construction as a kind of tedious corporate Mad Libs game.[118] We have all seen these kinds of documents and with

those words.

A "brand screenplay" needs a lot of detail and

clear choices that are not just positives versus negatives. Great words help put stakes in the ground. Good screenplay dialogue needs that deeper meaning. Remember, anywhere that you don't have detail or stories to back a word up, the more you will have to let people fill in the blanks on their own. If the words are weak, don't get upset if their interpretation isn't what you intended. Unless you have someone in your company who is on the "do not innovate" team, I am not sure telling them to innovate helps. Instead, explain what your company means by "innovation" through inspiring stories.

3. The story sounds Pollyanna-ish or avoids reality.

For a long time, we have all realized that the business world is a tough place, full of challenges, hard times, struggles, and stock drops. Companies come and go, and brands thrive and disappear. Many projects work and many others fail, even when they have what appears to be a great idea.

This is reality, and brands or companies that avoid these realities can look inauthentic, if not insulting, very quickly. I am not suggesting that doom and gloom is the way to proceed, but I am telling you *not* to cover up the challenges and obstacles. Some companies call that "straight talk." That is fine; I call it honesty.

Share those failure stories and what you learned.

Display them, even! I created a display in the P&G museum that shows failed products, and it is a place where we share the stories of why they failed, what we learned, and how they have helped the company in future initiatives.

If you aren't failing, then you are not innovating! Don't cover those up, every employee should know them. Nobody and nothing is perfect, and that is what makes us human. All the stories we tell must sound human too. Embrace your vulnerability. Make your brand sound perfect and you will insult the audience. No brand is. Remember who they are made by—humans!

Humans aren't perfect; therefore, by default, the brand isn't either. Be honest, be authentic, and do not paint a picture of no mistakes. Admitting what your brand's strengths *and* weaknesses are can actually help show what choices you have made, what you believe in, and where you will focus. That is a far more interesting story than "our brand is the best and the world we live in is always sunny and warm."

Just watch some of the TV ads out there today and you will see what I mean. You can quickly tell which companies are embracing the chaos and unpredictability of the real world and the challenges that brings and which ones are ignoring it to try and look perfect.

4. The story is created in a day.

Don't let your story be rushed or seen as a simple checklist item. Watch out for the classic "let's create a large brand strategy in a day" syndrome. Always remember, you get back what you put in. If you rush it, it will look and sound rushed.

Execution work is *not* a meeting—it is the project and potentially the future of your company. Treat it that way. Building strategy is not something wedged in between your Monday morning department meeting and your lunch meeting with your manager.

Meetings and projects are not all created equal. You must know how to prioritize, even at the expense of one of your other projects. When it is time to create the big story, you have to make the time.

Unfortunately, businesses can develop what I call CADD (Corporate Attention Deficit Disorder). They have a lot of meetings scheduled, and everyone has multiple projects going on at once. That can create a lack of focus and patience, and it can weaken the willingness to do the work truly necessary to make a successful story.

I met with a team not long ago that was preparing for a yearly session. The objective of the session was to share their future brand plans with a key retailer. As they described what they wanted to do, it became clear that they really hoped to create the entire plan in this single meeting. I asked if they had a story, and someone said they did and showed me a list of brand attributes and benefits—a checklist. That is not a story!

What they wanted to create was a multi-brand story brought to life through an immersive 3-D experience that would not only excite and inspire the retailer but also show how unified the team was across the larger portfolio of brands. That is an awesome idea, but I had to caution them that one meeting wasn't going to do it, nor would two, or even three. I could see some of their eyes and smiles drop as I explained that it may take a lot of meetings and that the best stories take time. That nothing worthwhile is easy.

If you want to create something as powerful as a great story—like an award-winning movie for example, how often do you think a team like that meets? And with how many people? And how far in advance? And with how many edits and rewrites? Watch the end credits of a successful film and see the size of the team involved in a great production. Heck, look at the size of the team involved in a bad production!

Doing this right is doing it almost every day, as a team, until the job is done—not for an hour or two once a month. If you want to do it right, you may have to put something else on hold.

Part of the reason you need to be ready to give a lot of time is because you can't just turn on creativity. Creativity doesn't appear at your beck and call. It is like a cat. Cats come to you when they are ready (if only creativity were like dogs!).

As a designer, I know this to be true. Some days it would just flow, and others, nada. The right environment can help, but it is still no guarantee. So, you just have to work on it *every* day to increase the chances of catching that elusive creativity bug.

In McKee's class, he mentioned that he knows writers who literally chain themselves to their computer some days. You have to stick to it and keep trying.

Anytime a team sets up a single-day meeting with the objective of developing something they are calling "final" (especially if it will involve the unknown, creativity, problem solving, and strategic planning), please raise a big flag and be wary.

Of course, you do need to meet. You have to start somewhere, but once you are in the meeting you need everyone to focus. Session focus has also become a big problem, one that has become so commonplace now that it saddens me. You have to eliminate one of the biggest problems of all...the "multitasking fantasy" sickness.

Be a great audience for your colleagues

Great stories require both a teller and a listener, and both have to be *equally* involved. Multitasking is a fallacy. It is not possible. You can't do two different activities at the same time with the same quality (unless that quality is "bad" or "half-assed").

How has texting and driving been working out? It ironically seems like the number of idiots on the road grows with every technological advancement. This is why we can't have flying cars, or at least not ones driven by people. With the bad drivers on the road today, just think about them in the air! This is why autonomous cars are not a matter of *if* but a matter of *when*.

At a meeting where creativity is critical, you will need your team all there and all attentive. Collect laptops and smartphones at the beginning and explain that there will be breaks.

I have been to a company where, at the meeting room doors, they have a cabinet called "Digital Detention." A set of shelves that you can quickly put a first name by and park your laptop and phone. I try to make all of my workshops an "analog only" meeting—nothing digital allowed at the tables at all!

Have everyone try that old pen and paper thing.

Frankly, people multitasking, staring at laptops, checking phones, half-listening as they answer emails is just simply rude. Yes, all you people tapping on a keyboard as your colleague presents their content—a presentation that they worked hard on, that they were excited to share. They are now being unnecessarily distracted and get to see the sides of your face with an occasional look up. What a great way to show that collaborative spirit and respect.

This is a virus infecting companies everywhere. You are there to focus on a problem, and your team needs you to bring all of yourself to the table—not one eighth of you because you have a lunch meeting to prepare for. Hey, I know we can all get really busy. If you can't make a workshop, then explain it to the host and go work on your other project. That will give them time to find someone else. But if you go and have to take calls, check emails, and disappear throughout the day, it is not helping.

I believe in "meeting karma" too. You will get back what you give, so don't complain when people are rude to you, never look up at your slides, or leave your presentation early because they have four other meetings.

If I get pushback when I try to schedule more than a day for an important story workshop, I ask the project team a comparative question related to their discipline. For example, if I am talking to marketers, I will ask how many times they meet when they are working on the ad strategy for an upcoming thirty-second piece of copy. The answer is "a lot," weeks and weeks even.

That is just for a thirty-second ad that will be around for a few months. But they want to create a brand story that will guide all the company disciplines and all the brand executions and be a part of the brand for years to come…in a half day?

Be prepared to remind everyone that to create a story, a real and well-done story, it takes tremendous focus and time. Again, 10,000 hours. Rome was not built in a day, and great strategies are no different.

> Strategy without tactics is the slowest route to victory. Tactics without strategy is the noise before defeat.[119]
>
> —**Sun Tzu**

If some people on the team aren't prepared to commit their time, fine, then tell them to send someone else to take their place. If they say that they have to be involved, great, then tell them what involvement really will look like—the time needed, etc. Set the expectations.

This book is based on content and tools that I have been sharing regularly for over a decade now, and yet it has taken over three years of my life to write this all down. Literally hundreds and hundreds of hours of writing, sharing, and rewriting.

Be realistic on what it takes to create something

worthwhile. It takes time, period. If it were easy, it would have been done a long time ago.

Of course, you also can't seek perfection and drag something out forever. We have deadlines and need to put a period at the end of the sentence eventually. You would be surprised how quickly great content can be created when a team is committed and willing to focus.

Again, it's not quantity—it's the quality.

Stories require commitment and hard work

So, those were the four big watch-outs to keep in mind. Of course, there are more, many more, and you will find various obstacles and pitfalls in any story project or process. That is all part of creativity. Recognize them, embrace them, and fix them as they come up.

Talk openly with your team. Ask, "What kind of story are we really trying to create? A good one or a bad one?" Remind everyone that a bad story can be just as powerful as a good one. It can still say, tell, and inspire things—unfortunately, things that you don't want.

If a team doesn't look or act committed in creating a powerful brand story, and you, as a participant, can tell their hearts aren't in it, then what does that say about their beliefs in the project? What does it say about the leader who said the project was a priority? What does it say about how passionate that team is about the brand?

Trust me, it will show in the execution. It always does. Here is what will happen: a team lacking commitment, unwilling to spend the time doing it right, will still create a story. Businesses are very good at completing deliverables. But it very likely won't be what they really wanted or needed, and it won't have the personal ownership and emotion from the team that it needs in order to truly succeed.

Remember the old saying: *"Measure twice and cut once."*

The real scary part is that a bad story may actually get used and it could create confusing directions or, heaven forbid, drastically affect the brand's reputation.

Employee commitment always shows up in the execution. Products are the direct manifestation of the cultures that create them. Consumers only have products to tell them what the company believes in and stands for. They don't get to see all the internal strategy documents or understand the hierarchies or meet all the people or be a part of the development processes. What story does your ad or product say about you? Your company?

Remember when I talked about the power of time? If it is a good story, then people always find the time. If it is a great book, you will find the time to read it. If it is a great TV series, then you will find the time to follow it. If it is a great project, then you will find the time and you will enjoy it too, even when it is difficult.

Don't just do it because you are paid to do it—do it because you want to do it. Do it remembering that it will be part of your legacy, a story for which people will remember you. Make it a story that you are excited to share with your family or capture in your company archives.

Now, I am not suggesting that every project has to be fun. Remember, you have a business to run and it's tough work. But work doesn't always feel like work when you love what you do.

If you only are dedicated for the fun projects, you won't have much in your legacy. It's called work because it is work, hard work, and a challenge isn't supposed to be easy.

But as we have said throughout this book, the challenge is the lifeblood of the story. For that reason, projects that aren't challenging scare me—because it probably means there isn't much value or substance there.

WORKBOOK

Chapter Seventeen Questions

Question: What behaviors at your company can stand in the way of getting work done? What stories would you tell to help change that?

____

____

____

____

____

____

____

____

____

____

Question: What is some of your company's favorite corporate lingo? What could you change (or add) to these terms to make them more unique to your company? (E.g., how is your innovation approach different from your competition's?)

Chapter Seventeen Notes

CHAPTER EIGHTEEN

What Can a Bad Story Do?

We all know that stories can be an incredible power for good and inspire generations of people. Great ones can change you forever, but bad ones are equally as strong. A bad brand story can potentially do irreversible damage and easily change a customer's thoughts and feelings about your brand forever (and in turn their friends' and family's too).

Look at the trouble that Volkswagen got into in 2015 with the preloaded cheating software for diesel emissions in their cars. My wife owned one of those affected cars and she once loved it. Then she heard the news, and I can't tell you the disappointment she felt. That disappointment grew to anger very quickly, too, especially when she thought about getting rid of it and other dealerships told her that they "wouldn't touch that car with a ten-foot pole."

For her, their brand story went from one about

fun, lighthearted, and dependable German engineering to inauthentic and misleading information, plastered across every newspaper headline. Only time will tell what the long-term effects may be, but I know that my wife said she is done with them.[120]

In 2017, United Airlines was in a similar situation with how they handled a passenger in Chicago, dragging him off the plane. Many voices on social media did not think the apology made by company management was adequate. Boycotts sprung up everywhere because of it.[121]

Stories can stick, so you really have to make every one count. I have another story for you, and it is an example of the power a bad story can have.

A few years ago, my friend Matt was very excited about buying a new car. He had a long commute each day, so he wanted something small but fun. After a few weeks of looking around and test-driving different models, he chose a popular compact car by one of the biggest auto brands. This was a brand that he and his family had always been very loyal to.

I remember how excited he was to show me his new car. Matt had the car for about a week before the "check engine" light came on.

No big deal, he thought, maybe he had

not put the gas cap on right or maybe it was just a simple bug in the system. He took it to the dealership, they turned it off, and he drove away. A few days later, the check engine light came on again.

Long story short, it came on two more times, and on the fourth time, he took it in and told the dealership to keep it until they figured out what was wrong with it. They had it for over a week before letting him know that they had finally figured out the problem and that he could come in and pick it up.

Matt arrived at the dealership excited to get his new car back. While waiting for it to be brought around by a technician, he grabbed a seat in the waiting room.

He began to notice something interesting: this dealership had the most beautiful waiting room he had ever seen! Great coffee, WiFi, several TVs with various shows and programming, and comfortable furniture. It was a really nice place.

Now, don't get me wrong, I love the idea of a nice waiting room; however, here was the rub. This particular dealership actually advertised its waiting room on TV and how nice it was! They sometimes would barely mention the cars and just brag about the waiting room! What story does that tell? I don't think they thought that through, particularly in today's environment.

But, back to the story.

While enjoying his free coffee, a mechanic approached Matt and let him know that while they were pulling the car around, they had accidentally bumped it into another car. They now would need to keep it a while longer. Matt stood there absolutely dumbfounded with a mix of sadness and anger. They kept his car for an additional two weeks to repair the damage.

Once again, Matt got the call that the car was done and he could come back in and get it. He now had had the rental longer than the car he had actually bought.

I wish I could tell you that this was the last challenge my friend would face, and that this was the end of his upsetting story, but I can't.

After retrieving his car and driving it for a week, the "check engine" light came on yet again. This was now the fifth time. He took it back in, now angry, and told them to keep it again until they figured it out.

During the following month—that's right, *month*—Matt would call for updates, get the usual runaround, and even had to start threatening legal action. The usual response he would get from the customer service department was the clearly forced and scripted, "We are so sorry for any inconvenience."

Really?

Quick side note to brand customer service departments. When it comes to brands, services, or products, "sorry" only means something if you actually fix the problem (or at least try to). Repeatedly saying "sorry" over the phone (or in person) is a meaningless gesture and ends up sounding hollow and scripted.

Customer service reps have to be empowered to fix situations if they are to have any real role in a brand's story. Remember how the Disney janitor fixed my friend Steve's situation? That is an example of how to make employees part of the story.

On the flip side, I was recently dealing with a delivery company. My package was very late, and every time we called to find out what was going on, the customer service people didn't have any different information than what I could find online myself. They even admitted that! So what role did they play? I could also literally hear them reading from a script that was probably on their screen, and the word "sorry" was one of their favorites. That didn't help and left a customer service scar I will never forget. It did for Matt too.

Back to his story.

When he would ask the dealership what they were going to do about the situation, they pointed their fingers at the head office and said that they were waiting to hear back from management on next steps and possible options.

Matt was quickly put into a position of complete helplessness because he was stuck between two different teams within the same company—the local office and the out-of-state head office. And, worst of all, he had no power with either. All he kept hearing were the words "we're sorry," but saw *no* action.

They finally decided that they could not figure out what was wrong with the car, so they told Matt the best solution was to rebuild the engine in his car.

What was missing here? At no point did this dealership, or the larger parent company, offer my friend a new car—they never offered him anything at all. He had bought it in January and finally received the same rebuilt car in April.

My friend and his previously happy and reliable relationship with this brand has been catastrophically and systematically destroyed. Honestly, since he would inform us every other weekend or so of his continuing trials and tribulations, we began to despise the brand as well—and then I would tell other people his story and they would too.

I wonder how many people avoided both this dealership and that car brand because of my friend Matt's poor experience? This brand is currently saturating the market with an ad campaign on how many awards they win each year, not personal stories of why people love their vehicles—just awards they are given. Who sounds like the hero in that story?

Matt's story is a tragic one. Its transformation is from faith to anger and irreversible disappointment. It is also one about how a story can create ripples in a pond that can get bigger and bigger as they fan out, affecting more and more people's thoughts and opinions. This story was so strong that it ended up convincing another friend of mine (who was getting a new car) to avoid this brand altogether. Just imagine what Matt could have done with a tool like social media (he doesn't use that)! He could have kept a visual story log of each step, similar to the Toronto Dead Raccoon story. People may have followed and added to it for months!

Bottom line, my friend Matt will never buy from this dealership again, and he won't be buying that brand again either. The brand experience he was originally excited about has now become a scar in his mind that he still brings up today. At least now he can laugh about it—a little.

The theme of the story I just told you is that *"tragic stories are just as powerful and memorable as ones with a happy ending."*

You better always make sure you have a really good story across all your brand touchpoints and mediums. A bad one can reverse the effects of the good ones very quickly.

Simply put, stories are a force that can stand the test of time, change the world, alter history, inspire the future, and make or break your brand.

The power of a good story

About a hundred pages ago, I told you the story about my friend Steve and his trip to Walt Disney World with his daughters. Let me ask you something: who stepped in on that trip and saved the day? Yup, the janitor. You remember that because I made you care. The story made you care.

A negative story can do the same thing and with the same longevity. Sometimes even more so! One bad story can ruin ten good ones. Always ask yourself what story your brand is *really* telling with every move it makes. What is that story? What are the stories being told about your brand when you and your company are not in the room?

Stories stick, so you better make sure you are telling good ones. This is why the story has to be a part of the culture in your company, big or small. This is why you need to have an archive or a heritage center in your company to collect, protect, and share the powerful stories—to make sure they are displayed and used as culture tools and future inspiration, not just timelines. This is why you need a story department or a corporate storyteller inside the company that will keep up with the story trends, principles, and fundamentals and how they are being used, along with developing trainings across all your functions. This is why you can't send all your storytelling needs to outside agencies. This is why everyone in your company has to remember that they are each a powerful storyteller for your brand and that the stories they create and tell *matter*, today and tomorrow.

Being part of a great brand is such a wonderful experience with incredible people to learn from. Remind your teams of that. What story do they want to share at their retirement speech? Or, better yet, what story do they want their colleagues to share about *them*? Everyone in your company is, and needs to be, a storyteller.

WORKBOOK

Chapter Eighteen Questions

Question: What story is your brand telling people through its actions? Are those stories aligned with what your company wants to stand for? If so, how? If not, what needs to change?

Question: What bad brand story would you share internally to demonstrate the effect a poor customer experience in your business can have? What is the *theme* behind that story? How is that being shared across your company?

Chapter Eighteen Notes

CONCLUSION

Remember...

We have introduced a lot of material about one of the oldest and most powerful tools that human beings use—the art and craft of story and storytelling. Let me end by reminding you of a few key points we discussed:

1. *The idea of story is not a deliverable; it is a way of thinking and doing things; it is a form, not a formula.* Don't look at story as an algorithm. Story is an organic process, so be agile with it. Study it, learn it, and practice it.

2. *To truly learn about story, you need to study*

the industry that sets most of the trends in it, and that is the industry of stage, page, and screen. Watch the hits and the flops, keep a pulse on societal trends in the different story mediums and how they are being executed. Businesses need to understand, master, and use those trends. Movies and TV shows are part of the pop culture lexicon, and that is why you have to keep up with them. Use the story ingredients as a way to journal what you are seeing and hearing or what is working and what isn't.

3. *Always start with your audience, deeply understand your "who," what is out of balance for them, what they want, and what they really need.* It doesn't matter if you like your story; it only matters if they do. Create content that your audience loves and wants.

4. *Emotions influence decisions, and stories influence emotions, therefore stories have a lot of power!* Don't get too hung up on data, and if you use it, don't lose the emotion behind it! Story with data can be incredibly powerful, but either one alone in the business world can look shallow. It has to be head *and* heart, not head or heart.

5. *Want to raise an issue or make a point, tell a story about it!* Stories can bring about incredible change. We see it every day as new movements start. Stories are what people look for, follow, and want to be a part of. Your stories can change your company and even the world! What stories in your company or about your brand have made a difference? Examine and learn from those.

6. *Make me care.* If you can't, I won't. No one has time for bad stories anymore, so it better be good. If it's not, don't even bother. If it is a good story, people will care—plain and simple. Always be sure you are clear on what you want your audience to care about!

7. *The best stories are always told, never sold.* Show that you love your story and that you believe in it. "Selling" is an outcome, not the means. Be authentic. Show your passion, insight, and excitement as you tell the story, and it will sell itself.

8. *Understand and leverage the fundamental story structure—a hero must go through an*

obstacle to get to a treasure. Structures are like bones: we all have them but we also all look different, so it has tremendous flexibility in expression. This is a universal story structure, and it can help you plan and examine potential storylines. Also research the Hero's Journey and study the works by Joseph Campbell and Christopher Vogler. The Hero's Journey is an irreplaceable tool to understand human connection.

9. *Your story can only be as powerful as the forces of antagonism allow it to be.* The problem/villain/dilemma is the key to your story's power. It is also the key to extending your brand sequel. Solve powerful problems. A weak problem will equal a weak story. Try to avoid stories that deal with a positive versus a negative. Talk about and show the real dilemma, tension, and choices that need to be made.

And the last one:

10. *The audience, the consumer, the user is and must always be the hero.* Any company that creates a brand, product, technology, or service should always be there to serve their hero—the people who purchase, learn, and use their products. You are the mentor in the

> story. What you develop and what you create has absolutely *no* power unless the hands of your consumer are there to guide it, buy it, measure it, learn it, dispense it, upgrade it, and use it. If the story is an internal one, then the employees become the hero and the company is the mentor. If you are a manager, then your employees need to be the hero and you need to be the mentor. Companies and brands are mentors, and their job is to guide and inspire their consumers. To do so, they must also provide them with items that can help them deal with the obstacles they may face.

As Uncle Ben told Peter Parker in the Spider-Man movie: *"With great power comes great responsibility."*[122] Remember my Storyteller's Promise and the importance of *time*. As a storyteller, you have a great power, and you owe it to the people you connect with to take that power seriously and to make it worth their time, worth their mortality. That is the most valuable thing that they can give you. Inspire them and leave them wanting more. Never forget that.

I want to personally thank you for your time and I am honored that you would read my book. Now go have fun, create your legacy, and tell your story. Best of luck, and of course, *"May the Force be with you!"*

—Shane Meeker
www.storymythos.com

APPENDIX

Your Own Story Research Library

Build your own research library—beginning with three of Shane's favorites:

- ☐ *Hero with a Thousand Faces* by Joseph Campbell
- ☐ *The Writer's Journey* (third edition) by Christopher Vogler
- ☐ *Story* by Robert McKee

Then pick these up as well:

- ☐ *The Anatomy of Story* by John Truby
- ☐ *The Storytelling Animal* by Johnathan Gottschall
- ☐ *The Seven Basic Plots* by Christopher Booker
- ☐ *Steal Like an Artist* by Austin Kleon

- ☐ *Screenplay by Disney* by Jason Surrell
- ☐ *Wired for Story* by Lisa Cron
- ☐ *Creativity, Inc.* by Ed Catmull
- ☐ *Save the Cat! Goes to the Movies* by Blake Snyder
- ☐ Aristotle's *Poetics*
- ☐ *101 Things I Learned in Film School* by Neil Landau and Matthew Frederick
- ☐ *The Art and Craft of Storytelling* by Nancy Lamb
- ☐ *Shakespeare for Screenwriters* by J. M. Evenson
- ☐ *Jaws in Space* by Charles Harris
- ☐ *The Story Factor* by Annette Simmons & Doug Lipman
- ☐ *The Art and Craft of Storytelling* by Nancy Lamb

There are so many more! Start creating a research library, fill your shelves, take some classes, and keep up with the trends in stage, page, and screen.

REFERENCES

Notes

1. Kleon, Austin. *Steal Like an Artist*. Workman Publishing Company, 2012.
2. Lapointe, Valerie. "Your Unique Perspective." *Pixar in a Box* online class. *Khan Academy*. 2017. https://www.khanacademy.org/partner-content/pixar/storytelling/we-are-all-storytellers/v/video1-final.
3. Cunningham, Lillian. "Being CEO Doesn't Make You Special." *Washington Post*. May 21, 2015. https://www.washingtonpost.com/news/on-leadership/wp/2015/05/21/the-tao-of-paul-polman/?utm_term=.01d8b92186fc.
4. Campbell, Joseph, and Bill Moyers. *The Power of Myth*. Doubleday, 1988, p. 122.
   The Hero with a Thousand Faces is Campbell's original work that inspired *The Power of Myth*:
   Campbell, Joseph. *The Hero with a Thousand Faces*. Pantheon, 1949.
5. Campbell, Joseph, and Bill Moyers. *The Power of Myth*, p. 4.

6. Campbell, Joseph, and Bill Moyers. *The Power of Myth.*

7. Gladwell, Malcolm. *Outliers*. Little, Brown and Company, 2008.

8. Gladwell, Malcolm. *Outliers.*

9. MacKenzie, Gordon. *Orbiting the Giant Hairball: A Corporate Fool's Guide to Surviving with Grace*. The Penguin Group, 1996.

10. Procter & Gamble Company Archives.

11. Info compiled from:
Huspeni, Andrea. "Google's 20 Percent Rule Actually Helps Employees Fight Back Against Unreasonable Managers." June 7, 2017. https://www.entrepreneur.com/article/295372.
Mytton, David. "Can Google's 20% Time Really Work for Your Startup?" *VentureBeat*. May 13, 2017. https://venturebeat.com/2017/05/13/can-googles-20-time-really-work-for-your-startup.

12. Procter & Gamble Company Archives.

13. Shahrzad, Rafati. "What Steve Jobs Taught Executives About Hiring." *Fortune*. Time Inc. June 9, 2015. http://fortune.com/2015/06/09/shahrzad-rafati-keeping-your-best-employees.

14. Pleasants, J.G. (Vice President of R&D, 1955–1969). Procter & Gamble Archives.

15. Cavna, Michael. "Emma Coat's 22 'Storybasic' Rules for Storytelling." *Washington Post*. June 25, 2012. https://www.washingtonpost.com/blogs/comic-riffs/post/pixar-tips-brave-artist-emma-coats-shares-her-storytelling-wit-and-wisdom-on-twitter-followher/2012/06/25/gJQADaxd2V_blog.html?utm_term=.1bdd96e040c2.

16. "About Rotten Tomatoes." *Rotten Tomatoes.* https://www.rottentomatoes.com/about.

17. McKee, Robert. *Story Substance, Structure, Style and the Principles of Screenwriting.* Harper-Collins, 1997, p. 113.

18. Procter & Gamble Company Archives.

19. Bradley, Bill. "10 Hilarious 'Seinfeld' Stories You Didn't Know Happened in Real Life." *Huffington Post.* June 24, 2015. https://www.huffingtonpost.com/2015/06/24/seinfeld-stories-happened-in-real-life_n_7648326.html.

20. Ferguson, Kirby. "Everything Is a Remix." *Vimeo.* 2015. https://vimeo.com/139094998.

21. Gottschall, Jonathan. *The Storytelling Animal: How Stories Make Us Human.* Houghton Mifflin Harcourt, 2012.

22. Brownlee, John. "Watch Elon Musk Design a Rocket Engine like Tony Stark." *Co.Design*. Fast Company. September 6, 2013. https://www.fastcodesign.com/3016934/watch-elon-musk-design-a-rocket-engine-like-tony-stark. Kumparak, Greg. "Elon Musk Shows Off His Crazy Iron-Man Inspired Modeling Setup." *TechCrunch.* Oath Tech Network. September 5, 2013. https://techcrunch.com/2013/09/05/elon-musk-shows-off-his-crazy-iron-man-inspired-3d-modeling-setup.

23. Strauss, Mark. "Ten Inventions Inspired by Science Fiction." *Smithsonian.com.* March 15, 2012. http://www.smithsonianmag.com/science-nature/ten-inventions-inspired-by-science-fiction-128080674.

24. Scott, Ridley. "When Worlds Collide." *The Guardian.*

April 28, 2005. https://www.theguardian.com/film/2005/apr/29/1.

25. Aristotle. *Poetics*. 350 BC. Transl. by S.H. Butcher. *Internet Classics Archive*. http://classics.mit.edu/Aristotle/poetics.html.

26. Diamandis, Peter, and Steven Kotler. *Bold: How to Go Big, Create Wealth and Impact the World.* Simon & Schuster, 2015.

27. Procter & Gamble Archives.

28. Litherland, Janet. "Friday Inspiration—Story Quotes." *BrandyStory*. May 28, 2010. http://www.brandstoryonline.com/friday-inspiration—story-quotes.

29. Aziza, Sarah. "11 Badass Female Filmmakers Changing the Game for Women in Hollywood." *Bustle*. February 19, 2016. https://www.bustle.com/articles/140464-11-badass-female-filmmakers-changing-the-game-for-women-in-hollywood.

30. Murphy, Shaunna. "8 Heartbreaking Truths About Women Directors in Hollywood." *MTV*. Viacom. June 23, 2015. http://www.mtv.com/news/2193922/celluloid-ceilings-female-director.
See also: Syme, Rachel. "The Original Six: The Story of Hollywood's Forgotten Feminist Crusaders." *Pacific Standard*. The Social Justice Foundation. February 26, 2016. https://psmag.com/the-original-six-the-story-of-hollywood-s-forgotten-feminist-crusaders-54002cf57d0e#.g160728sw.

31. Aziza, Sarah. "11 Badass Female Filmmakers."

32. Setoodeh, Ramin. "How Women in Hollywood Are Finally Taking a Stand Against Sexism." *Variety*. October 6, 2015. http://variety.com/2015/film/news/hollywood-feminism-womens-rights-sexism-1201610580.

33. Geena Davis Institute on Women in Media. "The Reel Truth: Women Aren't Seen or Heard." https://seejane.org/research-informs-empowers/data.

34. Geena Davis Institute. "The Reel Truth."

35. Bloomberg. *Celluloid Ceilings: Women Directors Speak Out. YouTube*. June 19, 2015. Video.

36. THR Staff. "Angelina Jolie and Kung Fu Panda 2 Director Jennifer Yuh Nelson on Hollywood's Female Director Deficit, New Kung Fu Panda 3." *The Hollywood Reporter*. December 8, 2011. http://www.hollywoodreporter.com/news/angelina-jolie-kung-fu-panda-land-blood-honey-270225.

37. Morgan, Alecia. "Rey from Star Wars Teaches Young Boys About What Women Can Do." *Huffington Post*. January 19, 2016. http://www.huffingtonpost.com/quora/rey-from-star-wars-teache_b_9018312.html?utm_hp_ref=feminism.

38. Finche, David, dir. *Fight Club*. 1999. 20th Century Fox.

39. Fleming, Victor, Mervyn LeRoy, King Vidor, Norman Taurog, and George Cukor, dir. *The Wizard of Oz*. 1939. Loew's.

40. Clark, Bob, dir. *A Christmas Story*. 1983. MGM/UA Entertainment.

41. Reinhard, Keith. "The Future of Advertising Still Rests on the Art of Connecting Brands and Consumers." *Adweek*. February 16, 2015. http://www.adweek.com/news/advertising-branding/future-advertising-still-rests-art-connecting-brands-and-consumers-162937.

42. Keierleber, Mark. "6 Reasons Why Singapore Math

Might Just Be a Better Way." *The 74*. July 11, 2015. https://www.the74million.org/listicle/6-reasons-why-singapore-math-might-just-be-the-better-way.

43. Gardner, Andrea. "The Power of Words." Created by purplefeather.co.uk. *YouTube*. February 23, 2010. Video. https://www.youtube.com/watch?v=Hzgzim5m7oU.

44. Silverman, Craig. "People in Toronto Created a Memorial to a Dead Raccoon After the City Forgot to Pick It Up." *BuzzFeed News*. July 9, 2015. https://www.buzzfeed.com/craigsilverman/people-in-toronto-created-a-memorial-to-a-dead-raccoon-after?utm_term=.xcnlnMBENk#.eml2GLY6gN.

45. Procter & Gamble Archives.

46. Brunsman, Barrett J. "P&G's Chief Ad Man: 'Too Often We Produce Crap.'" Cincinnati Business Courier. *American City Business Journals*. June 30, 2016. http://www.bizjournals.com/cincinnati/blog/2016/06/p-g-s-chief-ad-man-too-often-we-produce-crap.html.

47. Apple Inc. "First iPod Commerical—1000 Songs in Your Pocket." Posted by kreftovich1. *YouTube*. August 25, 2010. Video. https://www.youtube.com/watch?v=mM6lnCC_ee0.

48. McAlone, Nathan. "This Man Invented the Digital Camera in 1975—and His Bosses at Kodak Never Let It See the Light of Day." *Business Insider*. August 17, 2015. http://www.businessinsider.com/this-man-invented-the-digital-camera-in-1975-and-his-bosses-at-kodak-never-let-it-see-the-light-of-day-2015-8.

49. Tide advertisement. P&G Archives. 1946.

50. Frost, Robert, and Hyde Cox. "The Figure a Poem

Makes." *Selected Poems Prose of Robert Frost*. Holt, Rinehart, and Winston, 1966.

51. Pepper, John. Procter & Gamble Archives.

52. Always. "Always #LikeAGirl." *YouTube*. June 26, 2014. Video. https://www.youtube.com/watch?v=XjJQBjWYDTs.

53. *Breaking Bad,* Created by Vince Gilligan. 2008□2013. Sony Pictures Television.

54. McKee, Robert. *Story Substance, Structure, Style*. p. 317.

55. Benchley, Peter, *Jaws*. Doubleday & Company, 1974.

56. Sun Tzu. *The Art of War*. Transl. by Lionel Giles. *Internet Classics Archive*. http://classics.mit.edu/Tzu/artwar.html.

57. "The Annotated Art of War (Parts 3.16-18: Five Essentials for Victory)." *ChangingMinds.org*. http://changingminds.org/disciplines/warfare/art_war/sun_tzu_3-4.htm.

58. Kershner, Irvin, dir. *Star Wars, Episode V: The Empire Strikes Back*. 1980. Lucasfilm Ltd.

59. Tolkien, J.R.R. *Lord of the Rings*. Allen & Unwin, 1954.

60. Poison. "Nothin' but a Good Time." Recorded 1987–1988. Track 2 on *Open Up and Say … Ahh*. Enigma, 1988.

61. Hayes, Doug. In Michael Hauge, "Story Structure: 10 Simple Keys to Effective Plot Structure," *Michael Hauge – Story Mastery*, September 22, 2014. http://www.storymastery.com/story/10-simple-keys-effective-plot-structure.

62. Lucas, George, dir. *Star Wars.* 1997. Lucasfilm Ltd.

63. Fleming, Victor, Mervyn LeRoy, King Vidor, Norman Taurog, and George Cukor, dir. *The Wizard of Oz.*

64. Campbell, Joseph, *The Hero with a Thousand Faces.* Pantheon Books, 1949, p. 23.

65. "Hero." *Merriam-Webster.* https://www.merriam-webster.com/
dictionary/hero.

66. "Mentor." *Merriam-Webster.* https://www.merriam-webster.com/
dictionary/mentor.

67. See Annual Movie Charts, 1995–2016, in *The Numbers: Where Data and the Movie Business Meet.* E.g., "Annual Movie Chart – 1995." *The Numbers.* http://www.the-numbers.com/market/1995/top-grossing-movies.

68. Cobb, James C. "What We Can Learn from Coca-Cola's Biggest Blunder." *Time.* July 10, 2015. http://time.com/3950205/new-coke-history-america.

69. McKee, Robert. *Story: Substance, Structure, Style.*

70. Munier, Paul. *Plot Perfect: How to Build Unforgettable Stories Scene by Scene.* Writer's Digest Books, 2014.

71. DiYanni, Robert. *Literature: Approaches to Fiction, Poetry, and Drama.* McGraw-Hill, 2004.

72. Cameron, James, dir. *Titanic.* 1997. Paramount Pictures.

73. Madrigal, Marc. "The One Word Themes of Christopher Nolan." *Story Punch.* January 2, 2014. https://storypunchpodcast.com/2014/01/02/the-one-word-themes-of-christopher-nolan.

74. Fleming, Grace. "10 Common Themes in Literature."

ThoughtCo. April 5, 2018. https://www.thoughtco.com/common-book-themes-1857647.

75. Usually attributed to Oprah Winfrey. Also in Nancy D. Solomon. *Impact! What Every Woman Needs to Know to Go from Invisible to Invincible.* Wiley, 2009, p. 198.

76. Tate, Christian. "Avengers Assembled: Mapping the Web of the Marvel Cinematic Universe," graphic. *Christian Tate*. http://www.christiantate.co.uk/?p=1247.

77. Schwartz, Terri. "Kevin Feige Talks About the Build Up to Avengers: Infinity War." *IGN*. October 15, 2016. http://sea.ign.com/marvels-the-avengers-3/108831/feature/kevin-feige-talks-about-the-build-up-to-avengers-infinity-wa.

78. Holmes, Adam. "Why It was Important to Include Wakanda in Captain America: Civil War, According to Kevin Feige." *CinemaBlend*. October 2016. http://www.cinemablend.com/news/1566620/why-it-was-important-to-include-wakanda-in-captain-america-civil-war-according-to-kevin-feige.

79. Johnson, Zach. "Chris Hemsworth Gets a Major Makeover in *Thor: Ragnarok*." *E! Online*. March 8, 2017. http://www.eonline.com/uk/news/834617/chris-hemsworth-gets-a-major-makeover-in-thor-ragnarok.

80. Campbell, Joseph, and Bill Moyers. *The Power of Myth*.

81. Cambefort, Yves. "Beetles as Religious Symbols." *Cultural Entymology Digest* 1, no. 2 (1993). In *Insects.Orkin.com*, Orkin. https://www.in-

sects.orkin.com/ced/issue-2/beetles-as-religious-symbols.

82. Campbell, Joseph. In Joseph Clarence Rost, *Leadership for the Twenty-first Century*, Praeger Publishers, 1991, pg. 7.

83. "Myth." *Oxford English Living Dictionaries.* Oxford University Press. en.oxforddictionaries.com/definition/myth.

84. "Myth." *Wikipedia.* https://en.wikipedia.org/wiki/Myth.

85. Michelli, Joseph A. *The Starbucks Experience: 5 Principles for Turning Ordinary into Extraordinary.* McGraw-Hill, 2006, p. 12.

86. Clark, Taylor. *Starbucked: A Double Tall Tale of Caffeine, Commerce and Culture.* Back Bay Books, 2007.

87. "Jonathan Young on Joseph Campbell, a Scholar's Life." Adapted from Jonathan Young, "Joseph Campbell," *Dictionary of Modern American Philosophy* (Thoemmes Press, 2005). http://www.folkstory.com/campbell/scholars_life.html.

88. McKee, Robert. *Story: Substance, Structure, Style.*

89. Howell, Park. "Great Business Leaders Think like Authors." *The Business of Story.* https://businessofstory.com/great-business-leaders-think-like-authors.

90. *The Qur'an.* Saheeh International, 1997.

91. Godin, Seth. *All Marketers Are Liars: The Power of Telling Authentic Stories in a Low-Trust World.* Penguin Group, 2005.

92. "Timeline. *Tiffany & Co.* https://www.tif-

fany.com/WorldOfTiffany/TiffanyStory/Timeline/Default.aspx.

93. Fox, Allison. "Stephen Hawking's PSA About Should Be Required Viewing." *Huffington Post*. November 30, 2016. https://www.huffingtonpost.com/entry/stephen-hawking-obesity-psa_us_583f04b8e4b04fcaa4d61c29.

94. Peng, Tina. "A Guide to the World's Healthiest Booze." *Esquire*. March 9, 2010. http://www.esquire.com/food-drink/drinks/g482/healthiest-alcohol-030810/?slide=1.

95. Haven, Kendall. *Story Smart: Using the Science of Story to Persuade, Influence, Inspire, and Teach*. Libraries Unlimited, 2014.

96. Aristotle. *Rhetoric*. Transl. by W. Rhys Roberts. *Internet Classics Archive*. http://classics.mit.edu/Aristotle/rhetoric.html.

97. Jones, Josh. "The (Urban) Legend of Ernest Hemingway's Six-Word Story: 'For Sale, Baby Shoes, Never Worn.'" Open Culture. March 24, 2015. http://www.openculture.com/2015/03/the-urban-legend-of-ernest-hemingways-six-word-story.html.

98. Aaker, Jennifer. "Harnessing the Power of Stories." *Center for Women's Leadership*. Stanford University. Video. https://womensleadership.stanford.edu/stories.

99. Small, Deborah A., George Loewenstein, and Paul Slovic. "Sympathy and Callousness: The Impact of Deliberative Thought on Donations to Identifiable and Statistical Victims." *Organizational Behavior and Human Decision Processes* 102 (2007), p. 143–153. http://opim.wharton.upenn.edu/risk/library/J2007OBHDP_DAS_sympathy.pdf.

100. Generally attributed to Mother Theresa. See, for example:
Slovic, Paul. "Psychic Numbing and Genocide." *Psychological Science Agenda* (November 2007). http://www.apa.org/science/about/psa/2007/11/slovic.aspx. November, 2007.

101. Dykes, Brent. "Data Storytelling: The Essential Data Science Skill Everyone Needs." *Forbes*. March 31, 2016. https://www.forbes.com/sites/brentdykes/2016/03/31/data-storytelling-the-essential-data-science-skill-everyone-needs/2/#103dce957ee0.

102. Mycoskie, Blake. In Ariel Schwartz, "Toms Shoes CEO on Social Entrepreneurship, Telling Stories, and His New Book," *Co.Design*, Fast Company. https://www.fastcompany.com/1776334/toms-shoes-ceo-blake-mycoskie-social-entrepreneurship-telling-stories-and-his-new-book.

103. Dunne, Philip. Backstory: Interviews with Screenwriters of Hollywood's Golden Age. University of California Press, 1986, p. 156.

104. Jones, Josh. "The (Urban) Legend of Ernest Hemingway's Six-Word Story."

105. Daskal, Lolly. "101 Greatest Quotes About Success and How to Achieve It." *Inc.* October 2, 2015. https://www.inc.com/lolly-daskal/101-of-the-smartest-things-ever-said-about-success-and-how-to-achieve-it.html.

106. Landau, Neil, and Matthew Frederick. *101 Things I Learned in Film School.* Grand Central Publishing, 2010.

107. "The Silence of the Lambs (1991)." *IMDB.*

http://www.imdb.com/title/tt0102926/?ref_=nv_sr_1.

108. Heath, Chip, and Heath, Dan. *Made to Stick*. Random House, 2007.

109. Brown, Marcel. "1000 Songs in Your Pocket." *This Day in Tech History*. October 23, 2001. 10/23/1000-songs-in-your-pocket.

110. Spielberg, Steven, dir. *Jaws*. 1975. Universal Pictures.

111. Scott, Ridley, dir. *Alien*. 1979. 20th Century Fox.

112. "Follow Your Bliss: A Collection of Joseph Campbell Quotes." *JP Morgan Creating*. September 26, 2012. http://jpmorganjr.com/follow-your-bliss-a-collection-of-joseph-campbell-quotes.

113. Vogler, Christopher. *The Writer's Journey: Mythic Structure for Writers* (3rd ed.). Michael Wiese Productions, 2007, p. 223.

114. Sorkin, Aaron. "Aaron Sorkin Teaches Screenwriting." Online class. *MasterClass*. https://www.masterclass.com/classes/aaron-sorkin-teaches-screenwriting.

115. Campbell, Joseph. *The Hero with a Thousand Faces* (3rd ed.). New World Library, 2008.

116. Gallo, Carmen. "Airbnb's Brian Chesky Leads a New Generation of Brand Storytellers." *Forbes*. November 20, 2016. http://www.forbes.com/sites/carminegallo/2016/11/20/airbnbs-brian-chesky-leads-a-new-generation-of-brand-storytellers/#203de8522ef9.

117. Rashid, Karim. "Method Dish Soap." *Karim Rashid*. http://www.karimrashid.com/projects#category_5/project_209.

118. Fishburne, Tom. "Mission Statement." Cartoon. *Marketoonist*. January 30, 2011. https://marketoonist.com/2011/01/mission-statement.html.

119. Sun Tzu, *The Art of War*.

120. Atiyeh, Clifford. "Everything you Need to Know About the VW Diesel Emissions Scandal." *Car and Driver*. October 24, 2017. https://blog.caranddriver.com/everything-you-need-to-know-about-the-vw-diesel-emissions-scandal.

121. Yaverbaum, Eric. "United Airlines Has a Bigger Problem Than You Think." *Huffington Post*. April 21, 2017. https://www.huffingtonpost.com/entry/united-airlines-has-a-bigger-problem-than-you-think_us_58fa4374e4b0f02c3870e97f.

122. Raimi, Sam, dir. *Spider-Man*. 2002. Columbia Pictures.

About the Author

I'm a child of the 1970s. My fascination with the power of story started with a love of movies and an epic and influential pair of heroes—Batman and Luke Skywalker. Both would show me the importance of adventure and that hard work, taking risks, and learning from failure were all instrumental in finding any worthwhile treasure. Many a day on a small farm in central Ohio was consumed with me dressed up in a towel-made-cape fighting the underbelly of Gotham or wielding a homemade cardboard lightsaber battling the forces of the evil Galactic Empire. My sandbox was a perfect Tatooine, and my electrical engineer dad's old oscilloscopes and computer punch cards made my crude Bat Cave computer come alive. All of the stories of my childhood would play a huge role in the person I am today.

I eventually packed my cape and lightsaber away and attended college at The Ohio State University, where I studied industrial design. In 1997, I graduated and started my career as a design manager at the Procter & Gamble Company. For fifteen of my twenty-two years there, I helped lead the design strategy and execution for billion-dollar brands like Tide, Gain, Crest, Olay, and Pampers.

I loved the world of design but always had a desire to try my hand in Hollywood. So, I decided to write a movie screenplay. After spending years studying, researching, and immersing myself in the worlds of Hollywood, mythology, and fairy tales, I began to understand a deeper human truth: that the art and science of story could be used as a problem-solving tool in any industry. Story was not just limited to the traditional venues of entertainment.

I began to look at brands, companies, and products in an entirely different way. Consumers became valiant heroes, and brands became wise mentors bestowing magical items called "products and services" that would help our heroes face the obstacles in their journeys. Story was a way to understand our hero, the everyday obstacles they face, and the treasures that motivated them to endure and move forward. The idea of story opened my eyes to a totally new world of creative approaches.

From there I developed StoryMythos, a set of presentations, tools, and workshops to bring to life all the story principles I had learned while studying my favorite movies and story masters like Aristotle, Shakespeare, Christopher Vogler, Robert McKee, and Joseph Campbell.

For over twelve years now, I have been sharing my content inside and outside the company, helping hundreds of teams, brands, and organizations develop the stories they want to create and tell—companies like Walt Disney, Starwood Hotels, Columbia Sportswear, American Express, Exxon Mobil, and Anheuser-Busch. I also teach graduate story-based classes at the University of Cincinnati's DAAP School of Design and the Illinois Institute of Technology's Masters of Design program. Some of my story approach is featured in Jonathan Cagan and Craig M. Vogel's book *Creating Breakthrough Products: Revealing the Secrets that Drive Global Innovation* (second edition).

Today, I am the Procter & Gamble company historian and corporate storyteller, where I research and share the stories and insights from the rich 181-year company history while also continuing to deliver my StoryMythos keynotes and workshops around the world. My love and understanding of this idea called "story" is now my career, and I continue to research it, turning what I learn into new methodologies and tools. My personal hero's journey continues, and just as when I was a kid, I continue to find most of my inspiration from the fantastic stories of stage, page, and screen.

About Speak It To Book

Speak It to Book is revolutionizing how books are created and used.

Traditional publishing requires thousands of hours, and then you're asked to surrender your rights. Self-publishing is indicative of a poor-quality product with no prestige. And neither model boasts results-driven marketing.

That's why we created a better option. Speak It To Book has the attention of the industry because we are disrupting it in a brilliant way.

Imagine:

- What if you had a way to get those ideas out of your head?

- ☐ What if you could get your story in front of the people who need it most?
- ☐ What if you took the next step into significance and influence?

You can accomplish all of these goals by writing a book. Plus, you can do it without having to use a pencil, and in less than one-tenth of the time!

Your ideas are meant for a wider audience. So step into significance—by speaking your story into a book.

Visit www.speakittobook.com to learn more.

Made in the USA
San Bernardino, CA
13 August 2019